FRUGALLY FABULOUS
Wedding Receptions

GAIL EARLY

ISBN: 1450529445
ISBN-13: 9781450529440

Library of Congress Control Number: 2010900735

TABLE OF CONTENTS

෴

INTRODUCTION

Thank you for choosing Frugally Fabulous Wedding Receptions *to assist you in preparing for your event.*

We have organized the following chapters to correspond with the steps we take when we help our individual clients organize their event. Prior to using each section, we suggest that you review the information once in its entirety and then proceed to follow the steps in the same order as listed.

Several worksheets require information contained in previously computed worksheets. Please complete the worksheets in sequence so you will have adequate information available.

Our clients frequently express the surprise of actually being able to relax and enjoy their party or reception. Being organized and prepared will allow you to experience that feeling, too!

For questions or comment please contact me @ www.frugfab.com

Join my blog http://doityourselfweddings101.blogspot.com/
for additional money saving ideas and additional recipes.

FREQUENTLY ASKED QUESTIONS

This will be the first chapter in your reference book for planning every step of your function.

Some answers in this section will be covered in more detail in later sections. For other's; this will be your reference

THE BEGINNING

Where do I begin?

We suggest selecting several dates that would be acceptable and then locate an appropriate facility that can accommodate your needs. Many times people select a date but then have a difficult time securing a facility that is available on that particular date. To avoid stress, allow for flexibility in the initial stages of planning. You can certainly aim for one preferred date, but, if your dream location is already reserved, you will know you have options, which will keep the stress level down.

Do I need a budget?

YES!. You can't know how much everything will cost until you start pricing individual items. But, please determine how much money you have to spend on your function before you start. It doesn't need to be exact, a rough estimate will suffice. We suggest an overall budget for the function, which will help determine how much you have to spend on food and beverages. Knowing that you are within your budget as you purchase items for your function will also help reduce stress, at least for the person signing the checks.

The standard breakdown for the budget is:

Reception	50%
Music	10%
Flowers	10%
Wedding Attire	10%
Photography	10%
Stationery	4%
Extras – at least	6%

But….the 50% figure is based on having your wedding catered. You are going to be able to reduce that percentage significantly. The food cost for a self-catered menu for a full meal including two meat entrees plus appetizers, averages about seven to eight dollars per person. This does not include liquor, but neither would the approximately thirty-five dollar price from a caterer for this type of meal.

Should I plan on a full meal, or just appetizers?
We have included the questionnaire we provide to our clients to help them define their food preferences. This is addressed in more detail in the following question.

How does the time of day and season affect the plans?
The time of day will determine the type of food you serve; a brunch would work well for a late morning weddings, while appetizers and hors d'oeuvres would be appropriate for a mid-afternoon wedding. However, a full menu of appetizers and hors d'oeuvres is generally more expensive and time consuming to prepare. The most economical meals are brunch, lunch or dinner.

The season will affect two considerations you will have. One of the most important could be the weather. If you have a summer wedding, obviously you can plan for your guests to go outside if they choose. Many of our summer functions had seating set up inside and out. We find it is a good idea to plan for a place for each person to sit inside, and then have additional seating outside. If space constraints won't permit this, please point this out to the DJ so he includes the outside guests when it is time for the toast to the bride and groom and cut the wedding cake.

The other seasonal consideration will be the fresh fruit and vegetables that are more abundant during certain periods of the year. We encourage our clients to use what is readily available to lessen the impact on the budget. In additional to being served in recipes, seasonal fruits and vegetables make wonderful garnishes and give a professional look to the food presentation.

How does the location of the reception facility affect our plans?

If the wedding ceremony and reception are not located in close proximity of each other, you will need to consider the travel time for the guests to reach to reception after the ceremony. And consider the interval of time the guests will be at the reception while the bride, groom and family members are being photographed. Beverages should be available when the first guest walks through the door of the reception facility. It is a good idea to have snacks or appetizers available during this period of time if there is more than an hour delay before the bride and groom arrive.

What resources do we have?

If you have friends and family you have resources. The key is how you utilize those resources. Some of our clients do the majority of the work themselves with a little help from a few friends and family members. Others have formed committees and delegated the responsibility to handle the various aspects of planning, shopping, cooking, set-up, coordination during the event, and clean up afterward. Our advice is get as many people involved as possible. This is going to involve more work than you anticipate. And we have found that friends like to be a part of your special occasion. The most successful, least stressful events we have seen are those where a large number of people were involved in making it happen. The attitude was more about celebrating a very joyous event, not making an impression on others. The sense of community felt during these occasions is wonderful, and it filters down to the guests.

On a side note, we notice that those clients who don't ask for help from friends and family members are usually so exhausted and stressed, they are not able to enjoy the function.

Our goal is to help you not only to save money, but to have the energy and peace of mind necessary to to be able celebrate with your guests, whatever the occasion may be.

THE FACILITY

How can I find a facility to rent?

- Let your fingers do the walking......
- Check under Halls in the Yellow Pages

- Call all the local Fraternal Organizations; e.g., the local Elks Club
- Check with local churches…Ask if they allow alcohol if you're planning to serve it.
- Check with your local city and county Parks Departments regarding facilities they rent out for functions. Also check with your local parks and recreation departments.
- Check with alumni clubs
- Botanical gardens
- Museums
- Art Galleries
- Historic Estate
- Or, consider having it at home if your guest list is not too extensive for the size of your home.

The local recreation hall might look bleak during the day, but picture it at night with clear miniature lights wrapped around posts and in rows across the ceiling. Bowls of floating candles on each table provide a soft illumination …..…

How far in advance should I rent the facility?

Yesterday!

Seriously, finding an available facility for the day you want could be the biggest challenge you will face. So, this is your first priority!   Our local clients actually stand in line to book their receptions at several of the city park facilities. If they aren't in line when the registration for the year opens they cannot book their wedding for a Saturday or Sunday in late June, July, August or September. If you have a year to nine months before the wedding takes place you need to get busy. If you have less than nine months, get on the phone now!

How big a facility do I need to rent?

Several things will need to be considered in the equation. First of all is the number of guests you have invited….how many do you think will attend? At this point we need to interject some very sad and disturbing information…fewer people will initially respond to your RSVP than you are anticipating. And this is the most common frustration voiced by our clients. So….you will need to put on your guessing hat and figure how many invited guests are actually going to attend. Aren't you glad you don't have to give a head count to the caterer at this point!

The next consideration is whether you want to seat the guests at round or oblong tables. Most rental facilities can provide oblongs. So if you want round tables you might need to rent them. They are available to seat 8 or 10 people. The rounds will provide a more intimate atmosphere. The oblongs come in 6' and 8' foot lengths and seat 6 to 8 people if placed end to end.

Space Allowance for 96 Guests using Round Tables
Allow for 12.5 sq ft per person using round tables.
To seat 96 people you will need a space 30' x 40' for 12 tables.

Add additional footage as indicated for each area:

5' x 20' for 2 oblongs 8' long, placed end to end for the wedding party (seats 8)

10' x 10' for the bar area

10' x 5' for guest sign-in table

10' x 8' for the gift table

10' x 15' for the cake table

6' x 30' for the buffet

10' x 20' for the DJ

Using the above stats, you would need a minimum of 2200 sq feet to accommodate 96 guests plus a wedding party of 8 and a dance floor.

To adjust for additional guests, add 10 sq ft for every round table that seats 8.

If using oblong tables, allow for 8.3 - 9.4sq ft per person
To seat 96 people you will need a space 20' x 40' for 12 tables and the same space allocations referenced above for all other areas.

What are the five key questions to ask the rental facility coordinator?

How early can we get in to set up?

Can we use tape?

Can we string lights?

Can we burn candles?

What time do we need to be out?

If you are using a facility in high demand, there is a good probability you will be renting a "package" that includes a specified period of time; any extra time will incur an additional charge. Refer to the Reception Schedule Form to determine how long your function will last. Allow a minimum of two and a half hours for **food** set-up.

The time needed to set up the room will be determined by the extent of the room decorations, the time needed to place linens on the tables, and put table decorations in place. We suggest having one team to work on the room decorations and another to put up tables, get linens on and place the decorations on the tables. Have men available to do the heavy lifting, carrying and stringing. But have a woman on hand to <u>direct</u> the show. Use the men to set up the tables as they can be very heavy; they can then help the women put on the tablecloths and decorations. Remember to allow time for everyone involved in decorating to go home to get ready for the big event. We would suggest starting to decorate **no less than three hours** before the event, preferably four....that way everyone has time to relax and get in a festive mood prior to the function.

If you are using a facility that is not heavily booked, you can probably gain access the day before to do the decorating. This is the ideal scenario, and it reduces the stress level for those involved in decorating. The people overseeing the food prep will still need to be there two-and-one-half hours prior to the start of the function.

The tape, lights and candle issues are usually oversights that rear their heads right in the middle of decorating. Unfortunately, rental facilities have had to deal with people who have done things in such a way that damaged the facilities; and now the rest of us are suffering the consequences. Many facilities won't allow you to use regular candles due to liability issues, but will allow floating candles in a bowl of water. The new battery operated candles are a new alternative which can provide a nice alternative to no candles.

Of course, you will need to know what time you need to vacate the facility. Remember, you are responsible for leaving the facility in the original condition. You probably have a sizable deposit put down to ensure that occurs; so, get a clean-up committee organized beforehand to pick up garbage, clear off and take down the tables, sweep the floors, and help carry out all the miscellaneous items that need to go home. The more bodies the better for this task.....we have seen rooms broken down and emptied out in as little as 45 minutes. If you can recruit a dozen people to pitch in to help, you will be finished in no time.

If you add the set-up time, length of the function and clean up time together, you will have your time frame for the rental period.

Many facilities will allow you to rent the facility by the hour if you exceed the agreed upon time length. But, if too much time goes by....you are likely to lose those people who might be willing to pitch in and help clean up.

Do I need additional Insurance if I rent a facility?

Be prepared to purchase an insurance rider from your homeowner's insurance provider. The rider will probably run between $25.00 and $100.00 dollars for a day's event, depending on your geographical location.

What does the Rental Hall Provide?

Some halls provide tables and chairs. Be prepared to supply everything else. Detailed lists of everything you will need to rent or bring will be covered as you work your way through the FAQs and continue your planning.

PLANNING

How much food do I need?

When you plan a meal at home you have one entrée, a vegetable, a starch and a salad.

But now you are serving a large quantity of people, and probably want to offer a wider variety. So how do you know how much of each to prepare? We have included a worksheet; **The Recipe Key** which will assist you in determining the variety of recipes to serve, depending on your guest count and the type of function. It also includes instructions to help you determine how much of each type of food you will need.

Should I rent linens, dishes, flatware, and glasses, or purchase disposables?

This question arises as a result of two issues: financial considerations and aesthetics. Financially it is more prudent to purchase disposables.
Aesthetically it is nicer to rent the real thing.

Is it possible to have an aesthetically pleasing table without spending a fortune?

Absolutely! By combining rental and disposables, you can achieve an atmosphere of formality suitable to your occasion and not blow your budget.

Linen tablecloths will add the most formal tone to your function. They average about ten dollars per table in our area, and could be more or less in your area. We have seen many receptions and definitely feel they add color, texture and depth to the room that cannot be achieved any other way.

One option is to consider renting linens and flatware, but purchase rigid clear plastic dinner plates and clear plastic glasses for drinks. Set the tables with the linens and flatware. The disposables will be placed at the bar and buffet and will not be notice-ably different. By the time the guests get to the tables with their full plates, the food and drink will disguise the disposables.

A second option would be to rent linens, champagne and wine glasses. Place them on the tables with a favor for each guest. Disposable plates and flatware can be placed on the buffet, again not detracting from the table. By the time the guests sit down to eat they will not notice the disposables.

For disposables we have found a website for a company with a wonderful selection of reasonably priced disposable linens, napkins, plates, glasses and flatware. Go to **cateringsupplies.com** and cruise though all of their selections for serving pieces, linens, glasses and flatware. They have a large variety of colors and prices to choose from, sell in quantities to fit every need and actually have a phone number and names for personal contact if you want to talk to someone.

How much should I budget for renting dishes, flatware, glasses and linens?

Of course, you have the option of renting everything.

There are different levels of quality for rental dinner and flatware but the glasses seem to be fairly standardized. The rental facilities in our area offer three levels of quality; the following price is for the medium quality.

The average cost for renting tablecloths, napkins, plates, dinner flatware, water glasses, champagne glasses, cakes plates, cake forks, and coffee cups for one hun-dred guests was over $900 in our area. This did not include chafers or any serving dishes for the buffet.

The price for purchasing disposables can run over one hundred dollars, depending on how many serving pieces you order, the quality of items you order etc. Of course, everything can go into the garbage, although many of the items are sturdy enough to wash and re-use.

Besides cost, what is the most negative aspect of renting dishes, flatware etc?

Two factors affect dealing with rental goods. It is more time consuming and awk-ward to deal with; due to its' weight and the fact that it usually wrapped in plastic for protection. So allow more set up time if you are using rentals because it takes time to get all that plastic off. The other issue deals with the fact that everything must be returned relatively clean. All the food completely rinsed off. And again, it takes time to rinse 100 plates, 200 glasses and 300 pieces of silver ware. If you do use rental goods please see the following section regarding hiring helpers. When we have helped clients with their functions, this is the most arduous task....and everyone is already getting tired. If the dishes are returned with any food particles on them the rental companies tend to add a fairly substantial surcharge to your bill. And if anything is broken, you will purchase that item at a highly inflated price.

If I rent dishes, how many will I need?

Caterers add 10% of the total quantity (total number of guests) for every item ordered.

You will need the following items:

Dinner Plate

Knife, fork and spoon

Wine or Water glass (We recommend ordering a large water glass, which can used for white and red wine also)

Champagne glass

Coffee Cups and saucers

Cake Plate

Cake Fork

Substituting disposables for the cake plate and fork is an option.

This is a minimal set-up. If you are serving punch you might want punch cups. We don't recommend using salad plates or forks if you are serving buffet style, it seems to make it difficult for the guests to handle so many items.

What kind of serving pieces do I need?

The recipes you select will determine the types of serving pieces you will need.

Hot dishes will need a chafing dish to maintain their temperature. If you are serving more than fifty servings we recommend renting a back-up "hotel pan" so replacement pans of food can be prepared and ready to replace any depleted pans. The most important contribution to the buffet running smoothly is to have large size serving dishes. The amount of food they hold will reduce the number of times a piece needs to be replaced on the buffet, which reduces the man power necessary to maintain the buffet. It might be tempting to have friends and family contribute bowls and platters from home, but this will lead to a constant disruption in the serving flow as these items will need to be replenished constantly.

Hors oeuvres, appetizers, wraps, and cheeses can be placed on large platters.

Footed glass cake stands stacked with wraps or appetizers will add dimension to the buffet.

Salads and cold vegetables should be placed in large bowls

Green salads are attractive in large pebble plastic opaque bowls

Fruits should be placed in wide shallow bowls

Breads and rolls work well in large baskets lined with napkins.

Vegetables are appealing laid on flat greens in large flat baskets.

Dips in medium glass bowls can be set in a large basket and chips added to surround the dip.

We suggest renting the chafers. For easy clean up use disposable foil pans. Two pans 10"x12", approximately the size of a sheet of paper, will fit perfectly in the regular chafing pan. They can go right from the oven to the chafer and can be easily changed. And they go right from the buffet table to the garbage can. Price large bowls and platters at Smart & Final and Cateringsupplies.com; they have some items that can be used more than once and are reasonably priced.

Check out Michaels or your local craft super store for baskets; many times you can purchase a basket for what it would cost to rent a platter.

You will also need serving implements for each dish. Plan on having two large forks or spoons for each dish you are serving. You can find nice serving sized implements at your local grocery or discount store for less than five dollars each. Although they are a plain design they are very functional and can be used at home after the function. Plan on purchasing several small ice tongs; they are ideal for picking up pieces of cheese or relish tray items. If you are serving a green salad we highly recommend using the one piece combo salad servers......they allows guests to serve themselves salad without putting down their plates to pick up separate serving pieces. And again, plan on one for each side of the buffet.

For a very formal presentation you will probably want to rent all your serving pieces.

If we rent, should we pay the extra fee for delivery and pick up service?
YES, YES, YES,
This will be one less thing to worry about on the morning of the big day. We have watched the volunteer crew standing around waiting for the best man to arrive with

the linens so they could get the tables set……forty-five minutes before the wedding was to begin.

And it is one less thing to worry about at the end; every one is exhausted and can't face one more thing that needs to be done.

An option is to have one person responsible for this function, but not the Best Man, please.
And don't give them any other responsibilities during the function.

We don't have room to set up a buffet, how can we still serve a crowd?

Sometimes you are in a facility or home and just don't have a space sixteen feet long and four feet wide. So, you set up mini serving stations at different points in the room.

This is also an excellent way to get people to mingle at smaller functions. Put an assortment of dishes at each station and provide smaller plates at each station. Note: allow for 3 times as many plates when you serve in the manner. This has worked well in private homes with over 100 guests. The increased guest count will require additional stations, but the same food selections can be placed in multiple locations. This concept also pertains to the beverages. If you have a small space, serve different beverages in different areas.

Can you modify a family favorite recipe to feed a varied number of guests?

Please see the **Ala Carte Services** section on our web site www.frugfab.com

How many servings are in a keg of beer?

There are 960 oz in a keg of beer = 7.5 gallons = 30 quarts = 70 ea 14 oz glasses

How much champagne do we need to purchase?

The book says that one liter of champagne will serve approximately 12 - 14 each 2oz glasses. I counted the glasses poured from one bottle at the last function we coordinated and found 16 glasses. I would recommend using 16 glasses in your computations. The 2 oz might sound like very little, but most people take the obligatory sip and set the glass down….and they don't pick it up again.

What should we serve non drinkers for the toast?

Sparkling apple juice is a favorite. There are also several types of sparkling grape juices available. We don't recommend the non-alcoholic champagne; the sparkling juices have a much better flavor.

How much help will I need before the day of the function?

This answer is dependent on your guest count, how many dishes you are preparing and where the dishes appear in the preparation schedule. Several dishes can be prepared ahead of time and frozen. Others will need to be prepared from four to two days prior to the function. If you can delegate the preparation of each specific dish to one or two people, it will make short work of the recipe list. However, the preparation schedule is spaced so it can be accomplished by only a few people. The quantities of food involved will necessitate a longer preparation time than normally anticipated; this is very different from putting together a family dinner for twelve.

How many helpers will be needed to get the food and buffet ready?

You will need 1 person for every 15-20 guests. If you have this many on hand for two-and-a-half hours before the function, they will be able to get the food arranged on platters, the buffet tables set up, the chafing dishes filled with water and lit, the beverages iced down, the coffee made and all the other endless tasks that need to be done. Remember to allow time for them to get to the ceremony if it is located somewhere else.

Should I hire someone to work the day of the event?

It is one thing to do the prep work, but the day of the event you want to be able to enjoy yourself. And you want your friends to enjoy the celebration also.

But how do you do that and still have a function that runs smoothly?

One option is to determine which areas friends can handle, still feel like they are participating and have a good time.

Bartending and cake cutting are two of these areas.

However, having a friend oversee the food during the function is a little more imposing. This is where we suggest that if it is financially feasible, you find a few capable people and hire them to oversee the buffet. The food platters, bowls and the chafers will need to be replenished as your guests serve themselves. And more importantly, after everyone is done eating and the function moves forward, the buffet serving pieces need to be removed, the food bagged and all the serving pieces washed and dried. The rental pieces need to go back in their containers and your pieces need to be packed and ready to be loaded into your car. This task can take up most of the "party time" of your function.

Where can I find extra help?

To help make this part easier for you, we have compiled the **Detailed Task List.** This list will provide instructions for your help for every step of what needs to be done prior to and during the reception. If you have someone who can read and follow directions, you can relax and enjoy your guests. Order the task list at www.frugfab.com.

Where to look for that someone?

Do you have a favorite waitress at a local restaurant? Ask her if she and a few friends would be interested in making some extra money. You can ask them what they would charge to help you for a minimum of four hours.

Call your local Technical Trade School or Junior College and speak with the head of the Culinary Department. The students in the culinary program are already familiar with handling food, and more important, they love doing it.

Recruit from the local college Home Economics Department – it is probably called Food Sciences, or something similar, now.

Call the local college employment department and have them enter a temporary job that would be posted for the general student population.

Ask friends if they know of anyone who might want to pick up a little extra pocket change.

Check with local temporary employment agencies.

Our clients pay an average of $10.00 - $12.00 per hour and we live in a medium sized city. Adjust up or down accordingly based on the size of the town or city where you live. And please plan on giving them at least a 15-20% gratuity as they are going to be working very hard.

But if that isn't an option, what do you do?

Recruit one friend to oversee the set-up, another to oversee the reception, and finally one more to oversee the clean-up. Many times you will have friends tell you "Let me know if you need any help". Keep a list of everyone that says that to you….and take them up on it. But, let the people that you have put in charge of the three areas take it from there. Pass on the names of volunteers, but let the coordinators work out when and what they are going to do. The **Detailed Task List** will give the three co-ordinators the information they need to assign every task. Unless a person has coordinated the flow of several functions they have no idea of what is involved. Because we have literally been there with our clients, we know every step to be taken.

How do you feed between fifty and three hundred people in a time frame that leaves ample time to cut the cake, have a toast, dance and party?

Organize, Prepare, and Plan.

1. All food for the buffet should be "plated" on the appropriate serving piece when the food service begins. Having all replacement pans or trays of food ready to slip in place is the key to keeping the service going.

2. Plan on extending the exposure to your buffet line as your guest count increases.

3. Our goal is to get all the guests served in no more than forty-five minutes. If one hundred guests are being served, the buffet line is set up so guests can go down both sides. If over one hundred fifty guests are being served, we recommend doubling the length of the buffet, serving from both ends; front and back sides and essentially have four buffet lines.

What is the most effective way to prevent a long line at the buffet?
If you have a DJ, or Master of Ceremonies, request that they direct traffic and instruct specific tables when to proceed to the buffet. We found that two to three tables going to the line at a time works well. You can assign table numbers to assist with this routine, or have the DJ identify a group of tables. Doing this serves two purposes. It makes it easier for the people with a full plate of food to return to their table, and it makes it easier for the helpers to replenish the food. It is difficult to weave between large crowds of people when one is carrying a hotel pan full of hot food.

What is the biggest problem with disposable champagne glasses?
The bottoms constantly fall off. But, we brought this up because we have a simple solution. Get some friends together with hot glue guns, or contact cement, and have a party. Put the assembled glasses in large plastic bags, close with a twist tie and they are ready to be transported to the site.

What is a good alternative to canned soda for small children?
Juice Boxes: The smaller children tend to take several sips of soda, set down the can and walk off. Juice is healthier, the boxes won't spill and the size is right.

Why shouldn't you serve both punch and soda?
If you serve soda, the punch will sit and then be thrown out. If you serve one or the other, your guests will be satisfied.

What decoration shouldn't be put on the tables?

Small pieces of glittery confetti look very attractive on the table, but by the end of the evening they will be on the floor….and brooms don't seem to be able to catch them.

What is an inexpensive, but attractive, center piece for the buffet?

A bread waterfall is so much fun. Use different sized plastic cubes to build multiple levels and cover with a separate small table cloth. Use a large basket on the top level to hold a variety of bread loaves with different shapes and textures. Or, a flower arrangement is also attractive. Place graduated sized flat baskets on each level and on the table, going from small at top to the largest basket sitting on the table. Finally, stack a variety of rolls in each basket and build so that each level is stacked to the next. Place bowls of butter pats close by. Voila!

How can I save money on the wedding cake?

This is another item that can put a big dent in the budget. It is very easy to find Cake Designers who feel their creations are worth no less than $4.50 to $5.00 per slice. But we are going to assume that you might want to find someone who can prepare your dream cake for significantly less.

Check the yellow pages for Bakers, although you will undoubtedly find the most elaborate and expensive here, you will also find the grocery chains and independents that make very good cakes for a reasonable cost.

There are always non-professionals who create beautiful cakes because it is their creative play. So, how do you find them? Let your fingers do the walking; check the yellow pages for craft stores that sell cake decorating supplies. Call them and ask if they know of anyone who makes wedding cakes. You might need to even go visit them to view their business card board. You are probably going there anyway to check out all the wedding goodies, so you can kill two birds with one stone.

Be sure and cut out pictures of cakes that appeal to you so you can show exactly what you want in order to obtain an accurate quote. Be prepared for the cost to increase if you want different flavors, more elaborate trims or specialty frostings.

Most bakers have pictures of wedding cakes they have created, or at least as examples of what they can provide. The "hobby" bakers tend to take pictures of most of the cakes they prepare for clients. And have those pictures in an album. By viewing the pictures you should be able to tell if the person you are interviewing is experienced in baking the style of cake you want.

The one positive side of the wedding cake situation is that your friends cutting the cake won't charge you the 1.00 -1.50 per slice cutting fee.

What looks beautiful on the cake, but is difficult to handle and isn't really that tasty?

Fondant frosting It has been very popular the last several years. However, it is extremely difficult to cut, tends to pull away from the cake slice and cannot compare to the taste of a whipped or butter cream frosting. We have seen more than our share of partially eaten slices of cake with fondant frosting sitting forlornly on table tops at the end of a reception.

How much time should I plan on spending in the kitchen the day before the wedding?

None, Nada, No Way. The food is going to be ready at this point. You might need to hand a list or two of errands to helpers; or the father of the bride, or the groom--especially if they need something to do to keep their minds occupied. But this is your day to catch your breath; go get a massage, a manicure and pedicure, or whatever.

Why shouldn't I use zip lock baggies?

We love baggies, especially the new 2 ½ gallon size, but, only those with a nice slide lock that can be moved across the top of the bag to securely close it. The zip lock bags cannot hold up to the demands of being handled, weighted down by other bags and generally abused without their zip unzipping. We are considering purchasing stock in slide lock baggies because they make storing and transporting the food so manageable. They should be saved and re-used to hold leftovers after the function.

How much food can I heat at the facility?

This is a crucial issue. Does your facility have a commercial kitchen, with four ovens? Or a commercial stove? If not, you might need to have some of the food heated by friends before the ceremony and kept hot until the reception starts. Some of our recipes can be heated in the chafers, and we have come across some clever ideas for the remaining food which is answered in The Big Day section.

How much liquor do I need to purchase?

The Beverage section at the end of the Recipe File will give you a bar set up to serve fifty. If you are having a specialty drink, plan on each guest consuming two to three 8 oz drinks the first two hours and then 1 per hour following that. Some guests will do just the opposite but it will even out over the evening. Unfortunately, at some point you need to sit down with your guest list and determine who will be drinking alcohol, wine or beer, soda, coffee or water.

What is the one beverage that everyone drinks?

Water, water and more water: especially in the summer. You need to plan on a minimum of one bottle of water per guest. True, not everyone will drink it. But those who do will drink several bottles. If your function takes place during the heat of the summer, base your purchase on 1.25 bottles per guest.

We computed the cost difference between serving ice water in rented pitchers with rented glasses on each table, and purchasing bottled water. The bottled water is less expensive, plus the pitchers require refilling, and you would need someone to do that.

What needs to go in my back-up box for the kitchen crew?

The tubs that you can buy at the big home stores are ideal for transporting all the odds and ends that the kitchen crew will need.

A medium sized tub should be large enough to hold the items you will need. This could be a good test for the groom. Show him the list and send him to get the tub…..see if everything fits in what he brings home. But if you don't need that stress, have him purchase a 12 or 18 quart tub. We use two….one for the serving pieces, the other for every thing else. A separate detailed material list; that can be checked as items are added, is included as a tool for your convenience. But here is the rundown; foil, plastic wrap, more slide lock baggies, scissors, heavy duty clear tape, cutting boards, good sharp knives, first aid kit, matches or flicker style long lighter, light weight disposable rubber gloves, paper doilies, large measuring cups, a pitcher, 4 large spoons and 2 forks for use in the kitchen, a heavy duty can opener, 2 cork screws (we suggest the simple restaurant type – the others tend to break), 2 extension cords, one or two small portable fans. Every dish towel and bath mat you own, and at least 2 hot pad holders. Aprons if you have them, visit Goodwill if you don't. Take 1 box of 35 gallon heavy duty black garbage bags, sponges, SOS pads and liquid dishwasher detergent. (Use the dishwasher detergent to soak any pans with heavy baked-on food – it uses an enzymatic action to dissolve the food and is slick)   Also throw in a few plastic grocery bags from your last shopping trip.

Where can I find the best buys on disposables, without buying packs of 1000?

Check Smart & Final, Costco, Sam's Club and **cateringsupplies.com** on line.
Smart & Final has recently changed their disposables line, and I think their selection is much more limited. Costco has a great deal on linen-like oblong table cloths. But, we are most impressed with **cateringsupplies.com** for the variety and price for very nice disposables.

How can I economize on the food?

Buy in bulk, buy on sale and freeze. Also, watch for coupons in your local newspaper.

Several of our clients purchased all non-perishable items over a several month span of time. They found it easier to manage the smaller numbers of items as they shopped, and the cash outlay was more manageable.

How can I economize on the beverages?

Buying soda on sale will usually will save you the more than purchasing in bulk. Consider purchasing a keg if you anticipate a large number of beer drinkers. The keg will be easier to handle than cases and cases of beer cans. It is also requires less space to ice down. Remember that you will need a large tub for it and the ice. We have included several punch recipes that our clients found very pleasing; the punch was refreshing and satisfying, but not too sweet.

THE BIG DAY

How do we figure the best layout for the room? Where should we put the buffet line, the bar, cake table and gifts?

Start with your buffet line; it should be located on the side of the room closest to the kitchen door.

If you are going to set up a picture for your guests to sign, or a guest book table, try to place them inside the room located in such a way that guests are not standing outside waiting in line to enter the room.

The gift table should be placed away from the entrance door. Sadly enough, we have heard of gifts being carried off because the gift table was conveniently close to an outside door. Also plan on having a basket for cards; a decorated closed container with a slot in the top is even better. So many guests are now giving money in lieu of a gift that a secured receptacle is a good idea.

The DJ should have ample room to set up speakers, his sound board and miscellaneous equipment. He should also be in a position to observe all the activity in the room. It is not uncommon for a DJ to use a wireless microphone, which allows him to move freely about as he is "hosting" the event.

If you have decided not to have a DJ, a MP3 player with a speaker system will work well. When you are on line, keep your eyes open for suggested play lists for wedding receptions. The most effective music play lists we have heard start slow with the Bridal party dance and progress to more energetic music as the event moves on. The older generation will enjoy dancing to the older romantic tunes….if the music mix comes up through the years during the course of the reception, every age group will be able to dance to music they remember….and then they will drop out as they tire and can't keep up.

The cake should be set up on its own table, preferably away from the buffet and areas with a high volume of traffic. Probably the most crucial consideration to the lo-cation of the cake table is the background behind the table. What is going to appear behind the bride and groom in the pictures when they cut the cake? Allow room for an additional side table for the servers to use when they are cutting the cake. Match the shape of the table to the shape of the cake for a balanced effect.

Definitely plan on having a table set up for the complete wedding party. If possible include each attendant's spouse or guest. It is nice if the guests can see the couple during the celebration. This can be accomplished by seating the wedding party, or featured guests, at a long table with their backs to a wall. Or, seat just the bride and groom side by side at their own small table and have the wedding party sit with the other guests. We had one bride who insisted that she didn't want to have a formal wedding party table. She and her new husband were able to find seats together at one of the guest tables, unfortunately by the time the wedding attendants were ready to sit down, there weren't any tables that had more than one open seat. We happened to be there and quickly put up another table for the wedding party so they could continue celebrating the occasion together.

The bar location is determined somewhat by the traffic flow. You will need to allow ample room around the bar so that there is space for people standing and chat-ting as they wait their turn to pick up a drink. I suggest putting several rectangular shaped tables in an L formation. Have soft drinks, water and white wine in one area and the beer in another. Allow room next to the wine for wine glasses and opened bottles of wine. We suggest starting out with two bottles each of red and white uncorked; if you leave the corkscrews on the table, the guests will uncork additional bottles as needed.

However, one of our favorite ways to avoid delays at the bar is to place the different types of drinks in different areas. Sodas and water could be placed in an area away from the beer and wine. You will be icing down large quantities of all the drinks in separate tubs so this is easy to do.

How much time do I need to allow for set up?

For the location: If you have been reading this from the top, you already have an idea. What we didn't mention previously was that not everyone committed to show up will do so. Please recruit extra help with that in mind. As one of my clients stated "You really knew what you were talking about" when only one of her five of volunteers showed up – an extreme case to be sure. If you have two to four men setting up tables and two additional people putting on table clothes you will have that part of the set-up completed in short time. Initially have two people putting up decorations, the four to six doing table set up can assist them after the tables are finished.

Cardinal Rule Number 1 – Don't even think about having female members of the wedding party help; it doesn't work. They want to help make everything look wonderful for the occasion, but their presence is usually needed elsewhere before they can complete their assigned tasks. This puts stress on your remaining helpers who have to scramble to finish the work.

Cardinal Rule Number 2 – Try to recruit the groom and groomsmen to help set up tables and do miscellaneous jobs several hours prior to the wedding. **Don't** depend on them to carry out the bride's wishes in terms of decorating details. It is not important to them, they don't understand why it might be important to the bride; consequently, it will be handled accordingly. This is a task for a good friend of the bride or bride's mother who is detail oriented.

For the room set up, the more the merrier. As previously suggested, have one crew to do table set up and another decorate. We have found that sometimes the father of the bride enjoys participating in activities that reduce the drain on his check book and keep him occupied as his daughter and wife go through the elaborate rituals customary for the big day. The main consideration is that everyone has time to catch his or her breath, dress, and make it to the ceremony on time.

The time for the food setup will be determined by the number of helpers you have recruited. If you one helper for every fifteen to twenty guests and use our detailed task list, plan on 2 ½ hours. We have helped do numerous set ups for our clients; allowing for the fact that we know exactly what needs to be done, this is the time it takes and the number of helpers it takes to do it. If you have fewer helpers, add additional time. We realize this time frame might seem excessive, but the time goes by very quickly, and there are many things that need to be done.

What is the most common problem in setting up and decorating for the reception?

People not showing up and general chaos.

Now that you know what to expect, you can plan accordingly.

Write down a list of helpers. Now add two more names.

Put one person in charge of table set-up – give them a time frame and task list.

Ex: Start setting up tables 10:00 a.m., 14 rounds seating 8 each.

Put one person in charge of decorating.

Ex: Place bowl with floating candles on each table, place napkin, knife and fork at each place setting. Place one water glass at each place setting above the knife.

The directions don't need to be elaborate; they are sequenced to help keep everyone on track. They will also jog your memory about other things that you might want someone to take care of.

Draw a rough sketch of the room lay out. Look at your room dimensions to verify that you have room for all the tables etc. Make sure that guest tables are not encroaching on the area set aside for the buffet, bar(s), and cake table.
Using the same diagram, look at your traffic flow areas. Can all guests reach their seats?
Remember, there are going to be bodies sitting in the chairs at those tables – and you can't compute space needs based on a chair pushed up to the table.

Test the space:
One of the most important tasks during the initial table set up is to set up one table with chairs, set up the adjoining table with chairs and then have one person sit at each table so that they are back to back. Do they have room to move their chairs in and out...can they get up? Is there room for someone to walk between their chairs when they are both seated? This attention to detail will ensure that your guests are comfortable.

How can we keep food warm until it gets to the reception hall?
If you have determined (because of limited resources at the site) that food will be cooked at home and transported the day of the event you have two options for getting the food to the venue:

One is to rent a Campro unit; which caterers use to transport hot foods. The biggest problem with using such a unit is that you must also rent the specific pans that are sized for the unit. The unit can be large and difficult to handle.

The other method, which we recommend, is the "Do it Yourself Method." Gather large ice chests, bricks and towels. Check that your pans will fit and stack in your ice chest. Sometimes you will need to use a small cookie sheet as a stabilizer between layers. Play around with your empty pans and make sure everything fits before the day of the event. Purchase a sufficient quantity of new bricks to fill the bottom of the ice chest. It shouldn't take too many and they run approximately fifty cents each. On the day of the event place the bricks on the lowest oven rack to heat while the food is cooking. Put a towel on the bottom of the ice chest, arrange one layer of bricks, stack the pans and then put a heavy towel over the top of the pans. Close the lid. This method will keep the foods at a safe temperature for several hours. Wrapping hot dishes in layers of newspaper and then a big bath towel will also hold the heat for short periods of time.

Tips - If you are using this method, **don't** fill the pans all the way to the brim; seal each pan tightly with heavy duty foil.

Why shouldn't we put the napkins and silverware at the beginning of the buffet line?

The fewer items guests have to hold while serving themselves the better. By placing the flatware and napkins at the end of the line, guests are holding only their plate as they proceed through the buffet line. If time permits, you can roll your flatware in the napkin and tie with a ribbon, and place all in a basket at the end of the line. The guest then picks up one bundle before returning to the table. Or, you can place each item of flatware in a separate basket. The guest then picks up each implement. This works well also, and takes only a few seconds longer.

How should we set up the food on the buffet?

First, determine if you will have a centerpiece. A centerpiece gives a very professional touch to a buffet and does not need to be expensive or elaborate. Use anything sturdy to create one high level, or multiple pieces to establish different heights, then cover with a separate tablecloth. We have helped set up centerpieces with flowers, candles, food, and the previously mentioned bread water fall. Borrow footed cake plates from friends, stack with finger foods and place on the different levels. Fill in around the levels with left over greens from your floral arrangement. Combine the different possibilities; the goal is to have an interesting combination of height, color and texture. Due to stability factors, we don't recommend placing foods that are served with a fork or spoon on a centerpiece.

The first item on the buffet table will be the plates. If you are serving back and front, place a stack of plates on each side.

Because we include a wider variety of types of dishes than normally would be offered by a caterer, we tend to place the featured dish first. One of our clients had us modify a family favorite recipe; we instructed them to place it first on the buffet so it would not compete with all the other dishes. Your buffet will literally be a visual presentation, and we emphasize aesthetics rather than rules. One thing we have found that contributes to the presentation is to have similarly *shaped* serving pieces; round and square edges on platters and bowls seem to throw the table out of balance.

If you are using a single high centerpiece, you could place the flat serving pieces first, then place items in bowls, then place the chafers on each side of the centerpiece, reversing the order of the serving pieces to the end. There isn't a wrong way to set up a buffet; by working with the colors of the food and the size and depth of the serving pieces, you can present an appealing presentation of the food. That is what is important!

Another aspect that contributes to the visual appeal is to avoid great expanses of tablecloth. Using oval and round dishes and platters can contribute to the presentation by avoiding the look of solders lined up for inspection. By turning oval platters at an angle you can increase your available space, while covering up that dreaded dead white expanse. If you are serving from two sides, using very large platters of food, you can use one large serving piece as long as guests can easily reach the food from both sides.

What is the most effective way to keep the buffet line running smoothly?
Two factors will ensure that your buffet runs smoothly:

Have all the food ready to be served when the buffet starts. Do not plan on having people in the kitchen setting up platters for replenishment after the buffet starts… they won't be ready when you need them. The exception to this rule would be if you are serving 300 people and have two back-ups completed when the buffet starts.

Use large serving pieces. They will hold the quantities of food that will ensure a large number of people will be served before the dish needs to be replaced. If you have 12 items on your buffet, and each dish needs to be replaced every five minutes, the help will not be able to keep up; something will run out and your guests will be disappointed they missed out on something yummy.

What can we use to hold ice and beverages so we don't look like we are on a camping trip?

Tubs!! Determine how many tubs you will need for water, sodas, and possibly beer. If you are ordering a keg of beer, verify that the vendor will supply the tub to hold the keg

You are going to want fairly large sized tubs because you will have a substantial number of cans and bottles to ice down. You should have one half of the total beverage quantities on ice at the beginning of your function. Designate someone to re-stock the tubs after the first half-hour and then again at one hour. And, you are going to use the tubs initially to transport supplies to your site. Once you have determined how many tubs you will need, send someone to the nearest home store to purchase them. Another option is to use the round tubs carried at Smart & Final. We favor the oblong tubs because they are easier to pack and can be used after your function to organize the garage. To cover the tubs for the function, purchase medium weight cotton fabric and long lengths of tulle. After wrapping the tub in fabric, put the tulle around the top part of the tub and tie in a large bow.

How much ice do I need?

Start with 2 lbs per person. If the weather is quite warm, the beverages are located outside, or the length of the reception is exceptionally long, someone might have to go for an additional ice run after several hours.

THE PARTY OR RECEPTION

How do you avoid a mob scene at the bar as people arrive.

Set up the drinks in different areas of the bar area. Have wine and wine glasses on a table a short distance away from the keg of beer. Have several bottles of wine un-corked and wine glasses set up so guests can pour their wine and move on. Have sodas and water in another area. Have the keg tapped and ready to go with mugs or large glasses close by.

If you have a friend tending bar instruct them to have several glasses poured and ready for guests to pick up as soon as they arrive. The bartender can continue pour-ing "ahead" as the guests arrive.

How do you keep the kids from sneaking food off the buffet before thyou are ready to start serving?

Have kid friendly snacks set by the drinks the children will be served. Purchase the new child themed disposable plates and fill a few with Goldfish crackers, cheese cubes, celery sticks and black olives. Find a small child sized table to set up if you are expecting more than just a few young children; they will gravitate to an area set up especially for them. The remaining disposable plates can then be used for the children at the buffet.

How much time do we need to allow for all the guests to get through the buffet line and eat?

We like to plan on forty five minutes to an hour and fifteen minutes maximum for everyone to go through the buffet and eat. The buffet should be set up so that everyone can be served in forty-five minutes or less, if possible.

When should we serve the champagne?
When should the toast be given?

The toast is traditionally given after everyone has finished eating. Getting the champagne poured and to the guests can be handled in several ways.

Should the champagne be passed by servers or filled glasses put on a table for guests to serve themselves?

You can set the table with glasses and have someone put an opened bottle on the each table shortly before the toast. The guests can fill their glass and then pass the bottle to the person next to them. Or, tie a ribbon around the base of one glass at each table. The DJ can instruct the guest with the ribbon to pour champagne for the guests at that table.

If you have sufficient helpers, you can consider the following options:

Have one helper in the kitchen uncorking bottles while the others go from table to table filling the glasses.

If you have several helpers you can place the glasses on a tray, pour the champagne and then have helpers go to each table to serve the guests. This is more time consuming, and it can tricky to maneuver between the tables and guests while balancing a tray of filled champagne glasses. We don't recommend this particular scenario due to the time involved and the opportunity it presents to for an accidental spill.

Or, set out the glasses on a large table against the side of the room, close to the dance floor if possible. Have two helpers fill the glasses. The DJ will then invite guests to help themselves prior to the toast. Normally the bride and groom are standing close by and the guests congregate around them. If you are considering this and don't have a dance floor, make sure you have adequate room. Following the toast, the bride and groom traditionally have their first dance with everyone standing near the dance floor. This scenario lends itself well to getting the guests involved in the dancing if that is an objective.

How much champagne should be poured in each glass?

Fill to three quarters of the brim. As stated previously, champagne is very rarely fully consumed.

How do we know when to cut the cake?

If you are having an afternoon reception, plan on cutting the cake shortly after the toast, as some guests will start leaving at that time.

If you are having an evening reception, you can plan for a different situation. We recommend giving the guests a little more time after eating; usually everyone is dancing and visiting, and they seem to plan on staying longer. We certainly notice less unfinished cake when a longer period of time elapses between eating and cutting the cake. In this scenario, plan to cut the cake 1 to 1-1/2 hours after the toast.

What three items must be handy when the cake is being cut, in addition to the plates and forks?

The helper should have a pitcher of water and paper towels set on the floor, under the cake table. The frosting can build up on the knife and cake server. It can be easily removed by dipping in the water and wiping with a paper towel.

Should the cake be passed by servers, or the plates laid on a side table for guests to serve themselves?

This is another issue that requires the consideration of several factors to decide which will work best in your particular situation. How much help do you have? It will take two to three people to cut and plate the cake. If you have additional help, do they have room to get around between the tables to serve the cake to guests? Another frequent item we have come across is the fact that many brides choose to have different flavors on each layer of their cake. If you are trying to serve each guest, having them choose between flavors can be time consuming. In this scenario, we recommend having a side table set up where the plated pieces of cake can be picked up by each guest. The guests can then select the piece that appeals to them. It also allows people to sample more than one flavor or have seconds. If some people appear to be busy visiting and the help is available, they can put several pieces of cake on a tray and walk around the room to offer cake people who have not yet served themselves.

How many people do we need to cut and pass the wedding cake?

Well, it appears we got ahead of ourselves when we answered the last question. Again, minimum two, preferably three. This is just to cut and plate the cake. Number one person is the cutter, number two is the plate juggler and number three is the conveyer belt. Number one cuts a slice of cake with her right hand, while holding a cake spatula against the left side of the piece of cake, number two person holds a plate at the cutters left and the cutter lays the piece of cake (with the help of a cake spatula) on the plate. Number two then places the plate on a tray or hands the plate with cake to number three, while holding the next empty plate at the cutter's left side. Number two also has to separate each individual plate from the stack during this process.

Number three places the plates on a large serving table or a tray. WHEW!

How do you cut a wedding cake?

Google "Cutting a wedding cake" and choose the diagram best suited to your cake.

What is the best way to get the guests to leave so that we have time to clean up the hall and get out on time?

Well, the reception has been a success, the DJ is fabulous and everyone is having so much fun that they don't want to leave. But, the bewitching hour is rapidly approaching, and you know you have to get the guests to leave. Having the DJ just announce the last song seems to leave people suspended without a sense of closing. You are going to plan ahead, and your guests will think it is their idea to leave. While the bride and groom are there and everyone is having a good time, few people are going to want to leave. So, even if they hadn't originally planned to do so, the bride and groom are going to say "Goodnight, thank you all for coming", and they are going to leave. We have seen this work successfully over and over again. Then the DJ can then announce the last dance, the evening winds down naturally and comes to an end.

How much time will the clean up involve?

Several things besides clearing off the tables will need to be considered. You had different people bringing in things over a longer period of time to set up. Now, everything, including the garbage, needs to be removed from the facility, which means it will need to be carried to a vehicle or garbage receptacle. Without organization, clean up tends to take much longer than necessary and feels overwhelming. The game plan is to have each person doing one task at a time instead of doing multiple tasks in steps.

This is another excellent time to have a committee set up.

We recommend setting up three crews
1. Kitchen
2. Pick Up
3. Transporting

And two to three designated deposit areas.
1. Garbage
2. Take Home
3. Rental Equipment (if applicable)

Set up one area **outside** a main door where all the garbage bags will be deposited by the Pick up and Kitchen crew. This door should be closest to the dumpster or garbage receptacle so the Transport crew can dispose of them easily.

Set up one area just **inside** a main door where all Take Home items will be placed by the Pick Up and Kitchen crew. This should be closet to the area where the receiving vehicles are located.

To ensure the least confusion, decide ahead of time who is taking home which items the night of the function. There will be leftover food, all the supplies from decorating, beer, wine and sodas, leftover wedding cake and the gifts. The parents of the bride and groom are not going to have the energy to deal with getting things home and then putting them away. They can take anything that is not perishable. The food can be put in tubs with the leftover ice, which will hold them through the next morning, when you can face dealing with them. If there is no ice leftover, all food needs to go home and be put in the refrigerator as soon as possible.

The Kitchen Crew will be bagging or disposing of left over food, dealing with the serving pieces and cleaning the kitchen.

The Pick Up crew will be moving items from the hall to the designated door where the transport team will pick them up.

The Transporting crew will carry everything from the building to vehicles, or the dumpster.

The Kitchen clean up and main area clean up will be occurring at the same time.

The Kitchen Crew will do the following.

- Bag or dispose of all left-overs. Use baggies and food containers, and then place food in ice chests, tubs, or boxes. Move to designated Take Home area as soon as possible. Pay attention to weight of boxes and ice chests….ask stronger people for help if necessary.

- Rental serving pieces should be rinsed clean and placed in appropriate containers. The containers should be placed in the areas designated for Rental Items

- All other serving pieces can either be cleaned and repacked, or scrapped and stacked inside garbage bags to be taken home to be properly cleaned. The latter is often a viable option if time is short and every one is exhausted. It feels much more manageable the next day, especially when most of the silverware type serving pieces, small bowls and platters can be put in the dishwasher.

- When the kitchen is cleared of all food and serving pieces, wipe down all the counter tops and stove. Place all wet towels in a plastic grocery bag

- Return all supplies to the Back-Up box.

- Place Back-Up Box and wet towels (collected in a bag) by Take Home door.

- Mop floor if required.

The Pick-Up Crew will:

A Consolidate beverages so tubs are available to pack with miscellaneous items. Dry out tubs with towels from kitchen.

B Two people collect all miscellaneous items (flowers, candles, and decorating supplies) in tubs and place in the Take Home area.

C If you are using rental linens, two people can collect all of them and put in the Rental location. Then have these same two people take gifts directly from gift table to the appointed vehicle.

D Have several people go through the room to collect everything that goes in the garbage.

- Have one or two people with a bucket sweep through first to empty all liquids from soda cans, wine glasses etc into the bucket.

- Have someone follow them with large trash bags; everything disposable gets collected at that point.
- If using rental glasses, have one person hold the rack and the second person place the glasses in the rack as they go from table to table.

E Have two people break down tables, and then two-to-four people follow behind them to put the tables away. When all the tables are broken down, everyone can help put them away.

Have four people fold and put away chairs. When all the tables are put away, everyone can help put away chairs.

F If the room needs to be swept, someone can start on that task when a portion of the room is clear. Usually rental facilities don't require that you mop the floor in the main room unless soda or cake has been spilled.

Using the above method, allow 1 to 1-1/2 hours to complete the clean up.

You will need a minimum of twenty people:
- Three to four people for kitchen clean up. If using rental plates, flatware etc and you didn't hire extra help, plan on four more people to handle the rental pieces.
- Two people to collect rental linen and then take gifts to the car
- Four people clean off tables and pick up garbage in the main room.
- If using rental glasses plan on two additional people to place in receptacle
- Four to six people to break down and put away tables
- Four people to fold and put away chairs
- Four people to transport items from facility to vehicles and garbage containers
- You will be finished before you know it!

THE EVALUATION

The evaluation is a process. It is the first step in considering your resources and menu considerations. After completing the Evaluation, use the information to help you make decisions as you plan your event.

What time will event take place?

How many hours will your function last?

How many guests do you expect?

Is your function indoors with a kitchen facility?

Is your function outdoors?   Is there an electrical hook-up?

Are you renting dishes?   Or Use disposables?
Are you renting flatware?   Or Use disposables?
Are you renting glasses?   Or Use disposables?
Are you renting linens?   Or Use disposables?

Please review the following list of food categories

This is just to help define what type of food you do or do not want to have.

Based on the number of guests, we will help you determine how many types of dishes and the quantity of each that you will need.

After reviewing the complete list, rank the disability of each (1 being the most appealing).

Canapés, appetizers	1 2 3 4 5
Spread and Dips for Crackers/Chips	1 2 3 4 5
Cold Cut Meat & Cheese Trays	1 2 3 4 5
Sandwich Style Wraps	1 2 3 4 5
Meat(s)	1 2 3 4 5
Meat Casserole	1 2 3 4 5
Pasta or Potatoes (Hot)	1 2 3 4 5
Vegetable or Vegetable Casserole	1 2 3 4 5
Green Salad	1 2 3 4 5
Fruit Salad	1 2 3 4 5
Potato Salad	1 2 3 4 5
Pasta Salad	1 2 3 4 5
Vegetable Salad	1 2 3 4 5
Molded Salad	1 2 3 4 5
Chicken Salad	1 2 3 4 5
Vegetable Tray & Dip	1 2 3 4 5
Relish Tray	1 2 3 4 5
Barbeque	1 2 3 4 5

TIME EVALUATION

Don't forget to include the time of friends or family who will be helping you.

How much time will you have to prepare food two to three weeks prior to your event?

Several hours	☐
One whole day	☐
More than eight hours	☐

How much time will you have to prepare food two to three days prior to your event?

Several hours in blocks	☐
One whole day	☐

Do you have time to select and purchase the prepared food from outside sources, or someone who can do it for you?
Do you want to order it and have someone pick it up?

SPACE EVALUATION

How many refrigerators do you have?　　＿＿＿＿＿＿＿＿＿＿＿＿＿＿

How much freezer space do you have?　　＿＿＿＿＿＿＿＿＿＿＿＿＿

How many ice chests do you have?　　＿＿＿＿＿＿＿＿＿＿＿＿＿＿

How many ovens at the site?　　＿＿＿＿＿＿＿＿＿＿＿＿＿＿

How many refrigerators at the site　　＿＿＿＿＿＿＿＿＿＿＿＿＿＿

Beverage Options

Mixed Drinks	Yes ☐	No ☐
Beer	Yes ☐	No ☐
Champagne	Yes ☐	No ☐
Champagne Punch	Yes ☐	No ☐
Non Alcoholic Punch	Yes ☐	No ☐
Alcoholic Punch	Yes ☐	No ☐
Soda Pop	Yes ☐	No ☐
Coffee	Yes ☐	No ☐
Wine	Yes ☐	No ☐
Water	Yes ☐	No ☐

CHOOSING THE RECIPES

Let the type of meal you are serving, and your guest count, be the determining factor in planning the variety and number of dishes you consider preparing

The Recipe File is arranged by type of menu item

RECIPE SELECTION

The following tables are arranged in sequence by the type of the meal; the first step is to go the appropriate table for the meal you plan on serving.

1. Find the column closest to your guest count.
2. Each item with an X in the column under your guest count could be included in your menu selection. In some cases you will select a specified number of selections from multiple choices; which are distinguished by **shaded** backgrounds and a grouping of the columns. A section with corresponding worksheets follows the tables.

These tables are merely guides; you have the freedom to compose recipe combinations in any manner that appeals to you. Using the Recipe Quantity table and worksheets will help you determine the quantities of each you will need to prepare, no matter how many, or few, recipes you select. A blank worksheet is also included for your convenience.

RECIPE KEY

E = Entrée	**S = Salad**	**V = Vegetable**
R/P = Rice/Pasta/Potatoes	**A = Appetizer**	**F = Fruit** **C = Cheese**
RT = Relish Tray	**VT = Vegetable Tray**	**B = Bread**

BRUNCH SERVICE

Guest Count	25	50	75	100	125	150	200+
Menu Item							
Juice	X	X	X	X	X	X	X
Fruit	X	X	X	X	X	X	X
	Choose	**Choose**	**Choose**	**Choose**	**Choose**		
Sweet Rolls	2	3	3	4	4	X	X
Sweet Breads	from	from	from	from	from	X	X
Coffee Cake	these	these	these	these	these	X	X
Bagels	options	options	options	options	options	X	X
Mini Muffins						X	X
	Choose	**Choose**	**Choose**	**Choose**	**Choose**		
Strata with meat	1	2	2	3	3	X	X
Egg Casserole	From	from	From	from	from	X	X
Breakfast Meats	these options	these options	These options	these options	these options	X	X
Mini Quiche						X	X

LUNCHEON SERVICE

Guest Count	25	50	75	100	125	150	200+
Menu Item							
	Choose	**Choose**	**Choose**				
Fruit	**2**	**2**	**3**	X	X	X	X
Cheese Platter	from	from	from	X	X	X	X
Vegetable Tray	these	these	these	X	X	X	X
Relish Tray	options	options	options	X	X	X	X
Appetizer			X	X	X	X	X
Appetizer				X	X	X	X
Appetizer					X	X	X
Salad	X	X	X	X	X	X	X
Salad				X	X	X	X
Salad						X	X
	Choose	**Choose**	**Choose**	**Choose**	**Choose**		
Wraps	**2**	**2**	**2**	**3**	**3**	X	X
Meat & Cheese Platter	from	from	from	from	from	X	X
Mini-Quiche	these	these	these	these	these	X	X
Croissant Sandwiches	options	options	options	options	options	X	X

DINNER SERVICE

Guest Count	25	50	75	100	125	150	200+
Menu Item							
Entrée 1	X	X	X	X	X	X	X
Entrée 2		X	X	X	X	X	X
Rice/Pasta 1	X	X	X	X	X	X	X
Rice/Pasta 2						X	X
Salad 1	X	X	X	X	X	X	X
Salad 2			X	X	X	X	X
Salad 3					X	X	X
Vegetable 1	X	X	X	X	X	X	X
Vegetable 2						X	X
	Choose	**Choose**	**Choose**				
Fruit	2	2	3	X	X	X	X
Cheese Platter	selections from	selections from	selections from	X	X	X	X
Vegetable Tray	these	these	these	X	X	X	X
Relish Tray	options	options	options	X	X	X	X
Appetizer 1 Served before meal	1	2	3	4	4	4	4
Appetizer 2 Served as meal	6	6	7	8	9	10	12

THE RECIPE FILE

Over 70 recipes that we know your guests will rave about. We have already modified the recipes to serve 24 - 25 and have included worksheets to help you make modifications.

THE ENTRY FOR THE **"Multiplied X" COLUMN AND "Total Quantity"** COLUMN WILL BE COMPUTED AND ENTERED IN THE PLANNING STAGE, WHICH FOLLOWS THE RECIPE SELECTION.

Baked Brie with Caramelized Onions
36 – 40 Servings

Amt	Item	Multiplied X	Total Quantity
2 Tbs	Butter (1/4 stick)		
8 C	Sliced Onions (about 4 large)		
1 Tbs	Minced fresh thyme		
4 Ea	Garlic Cloves, chopped		
½ C	Dry white wine		
1 teas	Sugar		
1 Ea	8-inch-diameter 32 to 36 oz French Brie, packed in wooden box (reserve box) A different size of Brie may be used, adjust for number of servings		
2 Ea	French bread baguettes, sliced		

Instructions:

Melt butter in heavy very large skillet over medium-high heat. Add onions; sauté until just tender, about 6 minutes. Add minced thyme, reduce heat to medium and cook until onions are golden, stirring often, about 25 minutes. Add garlic and sauté 2 minutes. Add ¼ cup wine; stir until almost all liquid evaporates, about 2 minutes. Sprinkle sugar over onions and sauté until soft and brown, about 10 minutes. Add remaining ¼ cup wine; stir just until liquid evaporates, about 2 minutes. Add salt and pepper to taste. Cool (can be prepared 2 days ahead.) Cover and refrigerate.

On day of event, preheat oven to 350° F. Remove the Brie from the box; reserving the bottom of the box. Cut away only top rind of cheese, leaving rind on sides and bottom intact. Return Brie to box, rind side down. Place box on baking sheet. Spread onion mixture evenly over Brie. Bake until cheese just melts, about 30 minutes. Transfer Brie in box to platter. Surround with baguette slices

Yield – Approximately 60 servings

Notes: This rich appetizer is also lovely served alongside an assortment of crudités.

Recipe Key   A
Storage Key   R
Schedule Key   2
Utensil Key   Small Spoons

Chipotle Dip
3 Cups Dip

Amt	Item	Multiplied X	Total Quantity
4 Ea	Scallions		
4-6 Ea	Small canned Chipotle chilies in adobo plus ½ teaspoon adobo sauce		
2 C	Mayonnaise		
1 C	Sour Cream		
2 teas	Fresh lemon juice		

Instructions:

Finely chop scallions. Wearing protective gloves mince enough Chipotle to a paste to measure 3 tablespoons. In a bowl whisk together all ingredients with salt to taste. Dip may be kept, covered and chilled, 3 days.

Notes: Chipotle chilies are dried smoked jalapenos. They can be purchased packed in adobo, a sauce made from ground chilies, herbs, tomatoes, and vinegar. Serve the dip with bell pepper strips, chips, or crackers.

Recipe Key   A
Storage Key   R
Schedule Key   3
Utensil Key   Small Spoons

Creamy Shrimp Crostini
40 Pieces

Amt	Item	Multiplied X	Total Quantity
40 Ea	½-inch-thick diagonal baguette slices (2 – 3 baguettes)		
2 Tbs	Olive Oil		
1 Ea	8-ounce package cream cheese, room temperature		
½ C	Mayonnaise		
2 Tbs	Dijon mustard		
1 lb	Cooked shrimp, peeled, de-veined, coarsely chopped		
½ C	Minced green onions		
1 teas	Grated lemon peel		
1 ½ Tbs	Chopped fresh dill		
	Chopped fresh parsley		

Instructions:
Preheat broiler. Lightly brush 1 side of each baguette slice with oil. Arrange on 2 baking sheets. Broil until lightly toasted, about 1 minute.

Using an electric mixer, beat cream cheese, mayonnaise and mustard in large bowl to blend. Mix in shrimp, green onions, dill and lemon peel. Add salt and pepper to taste. Spread 1 tablespoon shrimp mixture atop each toast. Arrange Crostini on baking sheets; broil until shrimp mixture begins to brown, about 2 minutes. Top with parsley

Notes: Can be made 1 day ahead. Store toasts in airtight container at room temperature. Cover shrimp mixture and chill.

Recipe Key   A
Storage Key   R
Schedule Key   1
Utensil Key   Tongs

Ham & Cheese Wraps
60 Pieces

Amt	Item	Multiplied X	Total Quantity
30 Ea	Ham Slices		
10 oz	Cream Cheese		
½ C	Mayonnaise		
4 Tbs	Brown mustard with seeds		
2 Ea	Bunches green onions, chopped		
2 Ea	Small packages fresh spinach		
15 Ea	Medium Sized Flour Tortillas		
1 Lrg Can	Artichoke Hearts, sliced		
1 lb	Swiss Cheese, Grated		

Instructions:

Let cream cheese soften at room temperature. Mix cream cheese, mayonnaise/ Caesar dressing, and mustard. Spread cream mixture to edges of the tortilla, it should be thick enough that you don't see the tortilla surface. At edge closest to you, lay 2 ham slices on tortilla, lightly sprinkle with onion. Lay out several pieces of spinach and artichoke heart slices on top of spinach and sprinkle with shredded cheese. Don't try to get filling all the way to the end as the end pieces will be discarded when we cut the tortillas. Began rolling tortilla away from you, keeping firm pressure on the roll, and tuck in the side as you complete the roll. Wrap in saran. Wraps can be placed in a 9 x 13 cake pan to hold in refrigerator, however, don't stack too high or the weight will flatten out the wraps on the bottom.

Notes: Cut and arrange wraps on the day of the event.

Recipe Key   A
Storage Key   R
Schedule Key   4
Utensil Key   Tongs

Herb Garlic Crostini
30 – 40 Pieces

Amt	Item	Multiplied X	Total Quantity
1 ½ C	Cloves Chopped Garlic		
2 ½ C	Extra Virgin Olive Oil		
4 tea	Dried basil		
3 C	Grated Parmesan cheese		
½ C	Cream Cheese		
4 teas	Dried oregano		
2 ½ Tbs	Red chili flakes		
2 Ea	Sourdough Baquettes		

Instructions:

Blend all ingredients (except Baguettes) in a food processor to an oatmeal texture. Brush lavishly on Baguette slices. Bake in 325ºF degrees oven 1-12 minutes until golden.

Cool, place in freezer bags and place in freezer. Remove from freezer 1 day prior to event. Thaw in bag at room temperature.

Recipe Key   A
Storage Key   F
Schedule Key   3
Utensil Key   Tongs

Lemon-Rosemary Chicken Skewers
45 – 50 Pieces

Amt	Item	Multiplied X	Total Quantity
9 Ea	Skinless boneless chicken breast halves (about 7 ounces each = 4 lbs)		
50 Ea	8-inch bamboo skewer, soaked in water 30 minutes		
2 Ea	Pint basket grape tomatoes or small cherry tomatoes (50 total)		
1 C	Fresh lemon juice		
6 Ea	Bay leaves, broken into small pieces		
3 Tbs	Chopped fresh rosemary		
4	Large garlic cloves, pressed		
2 teas	Salt		
2 teas	Hot pepper sauce		
1 C	Light mayonnaise		

Instructions:

Cut each chicken breast half lengthwise into 6 thin strips. Thread each strip completely onto 1 skewer, leaving ½ inch of skewer exposed at 1 end. Press 1 grape tomato onto end of skewer. Divide skewers between two 15x10x2-inch glass baking dishes, stacking skewers if necessary.

Pour oil into bowl. Whisk in next 6 ingredients. Pour marinade over chicken. Marinate 1 hour at room temperature, turning often, or cover and chill overnight.

Preheat oven to 425ºF. Remove skewers from marinade and arrange on 2 large rimmed baking sheets: reserve marinade. Bake chicken until just cooked through, about 8 minutes. Transfer to platter.

Transfer reserved marinade to medium saucepan. Boil over medium-high heat 1 minute. Cool marinade 15 minutes. Strain. Pour ½ cup marinade into medium bowl; whish in mayonnaise. Season remaining marinade over chicken to moisten. Serve chicken with sauce.

Notes: Marinade can be made 5 days prior to your event. Keep refrigerated.

Recipe Key   A
Storage Key   R
Schedule Key   1/2

Meshwiya
4 Cups Dip

This recipe was introduced to us by a friend who had a party prior to leaving for teaching post in Tunisia. She served several Tunisian dishes and this was a favorite. It is very subtle and a perfect accompaniment to hummus and pita bread or pita chips.

Amt	Item	Multiplied X	Total Quantity
25 Ea	Tomatoes		
6 Ea	Green bell peppers		
6 teas	Salt		
6 Tbs	Cumin		
12 Ea	Cloves Garlic		
6 Tbs	Lemon juice		
1 ½ C	Olive Oil		

Instructions:
Traditionally, the tomato and pepper skins are removed by grilling over an open flame. If you want to peel your vegetables, dip them into boiling water for a minute or so, and follow with a lunge into cold water. The skins should slip off fairly easily. Chop the peeled tomatoes and pepper in to small chunks.

Add the salt, cumin and crushed garlic. Store the mixture, covered in the refrigerator. Before serving, add lemon juice and oil.

Notes: Served as a dip, or spread on small chunks of baguettes. Prepare with vine-ripened tomatoes for the ultimate flavor.

Recipe Key   A
Storage Key   R
Schedule Key   2
Utensil Key   Small Spoons or Tongs

Mexican Clam Dip
8 Cups Dip

When we found this recipe online, the comments were consistent that there are never any leftovers of this dip. The first occasion one of our clients served the dip involved a party with appetizers, a full buffet and desert. As the buffet was being broken down following dinner, I noticed a half of a pan of the dip sitting on the bar. I thought – well, so much for that. Right about that time one of the guests came into the kitchen grabbed the remaining dip and a bowl of chips….looking over her shoulder as she headed toward the living room she said, "We aren't done with this yet" The dip was gone by the end of the evening.
So, they didn't lie. It is simple, unique and delicious!

Amt	Item	Multiplied X	Total Quantity
24 oz.	Cream Cheese, Room temperature		
1 ½ C	(About 12 ounces) purchased green chili salsa (salsa Verde)		
2ea 4- oz.	Canned diced green chilies		
1 C	Chopped fresh cilantro		
6 Ea	6.5 ounce cans chopped clams, drained well, or use larger cans of clams available at Smart & Final 39 to 40 oz total		
2 Large	Bags Corn chips or tortilla chips		

Instructions:
Beat cream cheese in large bowl until smooth. Mix in salsa, chilies and cilantro. Add clams and blend well. Add salt and pepper to taste. Transfer to ovenproof dish. (You can prepare 1 day ahead. Cover: chill.)
Preheat oven to 350ºF. Bake dip uncovered until heated through and bubbling around edges, about 35 minutes. Or microwave on med-high heat for 8-12 minutes.
Place bowl of dip on platter. Surround with chips and serve.

Recipe Key   A
Storage Key   R
Schedule Key   1
Utensil Key   Spoon

Mini-Quiche
24 Servings

This is one of the dishes that we recommend purchasing from the Costco, Sam's Club or Smart and Final. It is added to the menu for variety and ease....because you don't need to do anything.

These can be baked ahead of time, refrigerated and then served at room temperature.
We have had clients attempt to serve them hot, but they usually cool off by the time they are eaten. If you definitely want them hot, place layers in a chafer and reheat with the lid on.

Amt	Item	Multiplied X	Total Quantity
50 – 75 ea	Miniature Frozen Quiche		

Instructions:
Follow package instructions.

Recipe Key	A
Storage Key	F/R
Schedule Key	2
Utensil Key	Tongs

Mixed Antipasto

25 Servings

A beautiful presentation that is yummy!

Amt	Item	Multiplied X	Total Quantity
Marinade:			
3 Ea	Large garlic clove, minced		
6 ¼ Tbs	Balsamic vinegar		
6 ¼ Tbs	Red-wine vinegar		
1 ½ teas	Crumbled dried rosemary		
3 teas	Dried basil, crumbled		
3 teas	Dried oregano, crumbled		
¾ teas	Dried hot red pepper flakes or to taste		
1 ½ C	Olive oil		
9 Ea	Large carrots cut diagonally into ¼-inch-thick slices		
6 Ea	Small Fennel bulbs (about 4 ¾ pounds), cut crosswise into ¼-inch-thick slices (about 9 1/3 cups)		
6 Ea	Red bell peppers, roasted and cut into strips		
6 Ea	Yellow bell peppers, roasted and cut into strips		
3 Ea	12 ounce jar Peperoncini (pickled Tuscan peppers), rinsed and drained		
2 1/3 lbs	Black or green brine-cured olives or a combination		
¾ lb	Sun-dried tomatoes packed in oil, drained and cut into strips		
2 1/3 lb	Marinated or plain mozzarella balls (available at specialty foods shops and some supermarkets		
1 ½ lb	Pepperoni or Soppressata (hard Italian sausage) cut crosswise into ¼ inch thick slices and the slices quartered		
3 Ea	7-ounce jars marinated artichoke hearts, rinsed and drained well		
1 C	Minced fresh parsley leaves plus, if desired, parsley springs for garnish		

Instructions:

Make the marinade:

In a small bowl whisk together the garlic, the vinegars, the rosemary, the basil, the oregano, the red pepper flakes, and salt and pepper to taste, add the oil in a stream, whisking, and whisk the marinade until it is emulsified.

In a large saucepan of boiling water blanch the carrots and the fennel for 3 to 4 minutes, or until they are crisp-tender, drain them, and plunge them into a bowl of ice and cold water. Let the vegetables cool and drain them well. In a large bowl toss together the carrots, the fennel, the roasted peppers, the peperonici, the olives, the sun-dried tomatoes, the bocconcini, the pepperoni, the artichoke hearts, the marinade the minced parsley until the antipasto is combined well and chill the antipasto, covered, for at least 4 hours or overnight. Transfer the antipasto to a platter, garnish it with the parsley springs and serve it at room temperature

Recipe Key	A
Storage Key	R
Schedule Key	3
Utensil Key	Small spoons

Wild Mushroom-Chevre Crostini
48 pieces

Amt	Item	Multiplied X	Total Quantity
4 dozen	Baguette slices (cut diagonally ¼ in. thick and 3 in long.		
2 Tbs	Olive oil		
24 oz.	Fresh mushrooms (Choose about three kinds. Chanterelle, crimini, morel, oyster, porcini, shiitake, or common)		
2 Tbs	Butter or margarine		
2 Tbs	Minced garlic		
½ C	Minced shallots		
2 teas	Dried thyme		
½ C	Dry white wine		
½ C	Fat-skimmed chicken broth or vegetable broth		
2 Tbs	Balsamic vinegar		
	Salt and pepper		
8 oz	Fresh Chevre (goat) cheese		
2 Tbs	Chopped parsley		

Instructions:

Arrange baguette slices in a single layer on baking sheets. Brush tops lightly with oil. Bake on the middle rack in a 350ºF regular or convection oven until golden, 15 to 20 minutes. Meanwhile, trim and discard discolored stem ends, bits of debris, and bruised spots from mushrooms (for shiitakes, remove entire stem). Rinse mushrooms well and drain. Cut mushrooms larger than ½ inch into ¼ inch thick slices; leave smaller ones whole. In a frying pan over medium-high heat, melt butter; add garlic and stir often until fragrant, about 1 minute. Add mushrooms, shallots, and thyme; stir often until liquid is evaporated and mushrooms are well browned, about 10 minutes. Add wine, broth, and vinegar and stir to release browned bits; boil until liquid is evaporated, 4 to 6 minutes. Add salt and pepper to taste.

Keep warm over low heat, stirring occasionally.

Spread Chevre equally on toasted baguette slices. Use spoon to spread warn mushroom mixture equally over cheese. Sprinkle evenly with parsley. Serve warm
Notes: You can toast the baguette slices and make the mushroom topping up to 1 day ahead. Allow both to cool before storing. Keep toast airtight at room temperature. Cover and chill mushrooms; reheat in a microwave oven at full power (100%) stirring occasionally, 4 to 5 minute

Recipe Key	A
Storage Key	R
Schedule Key	1
Utensil Key	Tongs

Parmesan Polenta Pizzas with Slow-roasted Pesto Tomatoes
48 Pieces

Amt	Item	Multiplied X	Total Quantity
24 Ea	Roma tomatoes (about 3 oz. each)		
	Fresh ground pepper		
½ C	Purchased or homemade pesto		
48 Ea	Rounds (each about 2 in. wide and 3/8 in thick) purchased cooked polenta		
2 C	Grated parmesan cheese (About 6 oz; see notes)		

Instructions:

Rinse tomatoes, cut in half length-wise, and place cut side up in an oiled pan. Sprinkle lightly with pepper. Spread about ½ teaspoon pesto onto cut side of each tomato half.

Bake tomatoes in a 350ºF regular or convection oven until browned on top and slightly shriveled, 1 ½ to 2 hours (if pan juices begin to scorch, add a few tablespoons water to pan) Let tomatoes cool about 10 minutes.

Place polenta rounds slightly apart on an oiled baking sheet. Sprinkle 1 cup parmesan cheese evenly over rounds. Set a tomato half, pesto side up, on each and sprinkle remaining cup cheese on top.

Bake polenta pizzas in a 450º F regular or convection oven until cheese is melted and beginning to brown, 10 to 13 minutes. Let cool 2 to 3 minutes, and then transfer with a spatula to a platter

Notes: For polenta rounds, buy four tubes (about 2 in. diameter; 4 lbs. total) prepared polenta: cut into 3/8-inch thick slices, discarding ends. It's worth spending a little extra for high-quality parmesan cheese for this dish; grate just before using. You can prepare the roasted tomatoes for the pizzas up to1 day ahead; when cool, cover and chill.

Recipe Key	A
Storage Key	R
Schedule Key	1
Utensil Key	Tongs

Caesar Turkey Wraps
60 Pieces

Amt	Item	Multiplied X	Total Quantity
30 Ea	Turkey Slices		
10 oz	Cream Cheese		
½ C	Mayonnaise or Caesar Dressing (I like to use ½ both)		
4 Tbs	Brown mustard w/seeds (omit if using Caesar dressing)		
2 Ea	Bunches green onions, chopped		
2 Ea	Small packages fresh spinach		
15 Ea	Flour Tortillas		
I Ea	Large jar roasted peppers, slices		
1 lb	Cheese Grated		

Instructions:

Let cream cheese soften at room temperature. Mix cream cheese, mayonnaise/ Caesar dressing, and mustard. Spread cream mixture to edges of the tortilla, it should be thick enough that you don't see the tortilla surface. At edge closest to you, lay 2 turkey slices on tortilla, lightly sprinkle with onion. Lay out several pieces of spinach and place pepper slices on top of spinach and sprinkle with shredded cheese. Don't try to get filling all the way to the end as the end pieces will be discarded when we cut the tortillas. Began rolling tortilla away from you, keeping firm pressure on the roll, and tuck in the side toward the center as you complete the roll. Wrap in saran. Wraps can be placed in a 9 x 13 cake pan to hold in refrigerator, however, don't stack too high or the weight will flatten out the wraps on the bottom.

Notes: Cut and arrange wraps on the day of the event.

Recipe Key   A
Storage Key   R
Schedule Key   4
Utensil Key   Tongs

Roast Chicken-Chipotle Nachos with Cilantro-Avocado Crema

Purchase cooked whole chickens from your local grocery deli to drastically reduce the prep time for this tasty dish.

Approximately 75 pieces

Amt	Item	Multiplied X	Total Quantity
1 ½ C	Chopped onion		
3 T	Olive Oil		
1 ½ teas	Cumin seeds		
1 ½ teas	Dried Oregano		
3 to 5	Canned Chipotle chilies, chopped		
6 Tbs	Tomato paste		
3 Tbs	White wine vinegar		
6 C	bite-size shreds skinned cooked chicken (see notes)		
75 Ea	Corn Tortilla Chips (23/4" wide)		
4 1/1 C	Shredded Jack cheese (24 oz)		
75	Fresh cilantro leaves		

Instructions:

In a large pan over medium high heat, frequently stir onion in olive oil until onion begins to brown, 4 to 7 minutes. Add cumin seeds and oregano; stir until fragrant, about 30 seconds. Add chilies, tomato paste, vinegar and 1 cup water; bring to a boil, then reduce heat and simmer gently, stirring often, to blend flavors, about 5 minutes. Add chicken and stir until hot. Refrigerate chicken mixture.

On day of event put chicken mixture in a shallow oven proof container and sprinkle cheese on top; bake in 450ºF regular or convection oven until cheese begins to bubble, about 3 minutes. Remove from oven and top chicken mixture with Cilantro-Avocado Crema and garnish with cilantro leaf. Serve warm with chips

Cilantro-Avocado Crema (Prepare on day of event)

In a small bowl, mix 1 cup finely diced firm-ripe avocado, 6 tablespoons sour cream, 3 tablespoon finely chopped fresh cilantro leaves. 6 teaspoons lime juice and 6 teaspoons milk. Add salt to taste Make 1 ½ cups

Notes: Purchase a roast chicken from a deli: a 2-pound bird produces about 3 cups shredded meat.

Recipe Key   A
Storage Key   R
Schedule Key   2
Utensil Key   Tongs

Sesame Eggplant Salsa
4 Cups Dip

This dip is a modification of a dip served at the China Moon restaurant in San Francisco. The flavors are complex; each mouthful is like experiencing three or four separate taste sensations. Men love this dip.

Amt	Item	Multiplied X	Total Quantity
2 lbs	Eggplant		
¾ C	Packed minced green onions		
2 ½ Tbs	Minced fresh ginger		
2 Tbs	Minced garlic (bottled minced garlic is fine for this)		
1 Ea	Small Serrano or Thai chili, minced, or 1 teaspoon Chinese chili paste		
3 Tbs	Light brown sugar		
2 teas	Fresh lemon juice		
1 Tbs	Seasoned rice vinegar		
2 Tbs	Tamari or soy sauce		
1 Tbs	Canola oil		
1 ½ teas	Dark sesame oil		
¾ C	Chopped, seeded and peeled tomatoes		
¾ C	Packed minced fresh cilantro, plus extra for garnish		
5	Sliced green onions		
2	Pita Chips - Medium Sized Bags		

Instructions:
Cut the stem ends off the eggplants and prick well all over with a knife. Place on a baking sheet and roast for 30 to 45 minutes depending on size. Turn at least once while roasting. The eggplant is done when a fork sinks easily into the thickest part. It should be completely soft. Remove from the oven and when cool enough to handle, scrape the creamy pulp from the skin into the food processor. Pulse quickly just until the eggplant is pureed. Combine the minced green onions, ginger, garlic and chili in a bowl. Combine the brown sugar, lemon juice, vinegar and tamari in a small bowl and whisk to blend.

Place a large sauté pan or wok over medium-high heat and swirl the canola oil around to coat the pan. Add the green onion mixture and sauté until softened without coloring, about 45 seconds. Add the sugar mixture and bring to a simmer, stirring rapidly. Reduce the heat and add the eggplant puree. Stir well to blend and heat through, 1 to 2 minutes, stirring constantly. Remove from the heat and stir in the sesame oil, tomatoes, and cilantro and fold to blend.

This may be served immediately, but it tastes better if made 1 or 2 days before and refrigerated. Bring it back to room temperature before serving. Garnish the top with the minced cilantro and sliced green onion and surround with Pita Crisp or chips.

Recipe Key   A
Storage Key   R
Schedule Key   5
Utensil Key   Spoon

Sesame Pork
60 – 70 Pieces

Amt	Item	Multiplied X	Total Quantity
2 C	Soy Sauce		
1 1/3 C	Chinese Rice Wine		
8 Ea	Garlic Cloves crushed		
1 Tbs + 1 teas	Grated fresh ginger		
1 Tbs + 1 teas	Sesame Oil		
6 Ea	Small Pork loins		
32 Ea	Green Onions		
8 Tbs	Toasted sesame seeds		
4 Ea	Loaves French Baguette		

Instructions:
Combine soy sauce, wine, garlic, ginger and sesame oil.

If using large loins from Costco, split length wise in half (diameter of raw loin should be slightly larger than a baguette slice) Long loins can also be cut in half to fit into plastic bags for marinating. Place loin in glass dish or slide lock plastic baggie, pour marinade over loins, place in refrigerator for at least twenty minutes.

Grill – 1) Preheat grill on high for 10-15 minutes, turn off gas on one side; place meat on that side-close lid. Turn meat after about 10 minutes. Continue cooking until meat is no longer pink (20-30 minutes total depending on how large the loins are) When meat is almost done, re-light flame and brown loins on all sides. Wrap loin in saran or place in large baggie, refrigerate.

Slice green onions and toast sesame seeds for garnish
Slice pork in 1/8" slices
Cut baguettes in 1/2" slices
To serve; place bread slice on serving tray, top with pork slice, green onion and sesame seeds.

Recipe Key   A
Storage Key   R
Schedule Key   2
Utensil Key   Tongs

Spinach Artichoke Heart Dip
3 Cups Dip

Amt	Item	Multiplied X	Total Quantity
2 C	Mayonnaise		
10 Ea	Large Cloves Garlic (pressed)		
24 oz	Artichoke hearts (canned)		
20 oz	Frozen chopped spinach (2 boxes)		
16 oz	Kraft Italian blend shredded cheese (Mozzarella, Parmesan with seasonings)		

Instructions:

Drain and rinse artichokes. Squeeze out excess water and chop up. Defrost, rinse and squeeze out excess water from spinach. Make sure spinach is broke up. Add all ingredients to bowl and mix well. Heat up dip in microwave or pay until hot. Can be served in a crock-pot. Serve warm with your favorite chips, crackers or baguette slices.

Recipe Key   A
Storage Key   R
Schedule Key   2
Utensil Key   Small Spoon

Steak and Chimichurri Toasts
60 Pieces

Amt	Item	Multiplied X	Total Quantity
1 ½ C	Packed fresh parsley		
1 ¼ C	Olive Oil		
4 ½ Tbs	Red wine vinegar		
3 Tbs	Dried Oregano		
3 teas	Ground Cumin		
1 ¼ teas	Salt		
3	Garlic Cloves, minced		
3/4 teas	Dried Crushed Red Pepper		
3 ea	1-pound pieces flank steak		
3 ea	16-ounce thin French-bread baguette, cut into 60 slices		
	Additional olive oil		

Instructions:

Blend parsley, olive oil, vinegar, oregano, cumin, salt, minced garlic, and crushed red pepper in a processor until smooth. Place meat in large glass baking dish. Sprinkle with salt and pepper. Brush meat with 2 tablespoons Chimichurri Sauce. Cover steaks and remaining sauce separately and refrigerate at least 1 hour. (You can make 1 day ahead; keep refrigerated.)

Preheat oven to 450ºF. Place bread slices on a large baking sheet. Brush with olive oil. Bake until just firm, about 5 minutes. Transfer to large platter.

Preheat broiler. Transfer meat to rimmed baking sheet and broil until cooked to desired doneness, about 4 minutes per side for medium. Transfer to cutting board. Let stand 5 minutes. Cut each steak along grain in half. Cut each half crosswise against grain into 10 slices. Top each bread slice with 1 piece of meat. Spread each with some Chimichurri Sauce; place on platter. Spoon remaining sauce into small bowl and place in center of platter. Serve warm or let stand up to 2 hours at room temperature.

Recipe Key	A
Storage Key	R
Schedule Key	2
Utensil Key	Tongs

Sun Dried Tomato Spread
48 Pieces

This recipe was given to me by a friend…..it was a closely guarded secret recipe served in a very popular restaurant in the Biggest Little City in the World; Reno NV It is a complex mingling of flavors mellowed by the cream cheese. This is very unique recipe that our clients rave about.

Amt	Item	Multiplied X	Total Quantity
2 Ea	3 oz Package Sun dried Tomatoes		
1 ½ C	Rice Wine, White Wine or wine vinegar (or combination)		
1 1/3 C	Olive oil		
2 Tbs	White wine		
8 Ea	Garlic cloves minced		
4 Tbs	Parmesan Cheese, grated		
12 Ea	Capers (I just drain & throw in a small bottle)		
12 Ea	Peppercorns		
2 teas	Basil, dried		
1 teas	Oregano, dried		
0.5 teas	Thyme, dried		
0.5 teas	Tarragon, dried		
0.5 teas	Parsley, dried		
0.5 teas	Marjoram, dried		
3 Ea	Cream cheese bricks		
4 Ea	Boxes Breton or Carr's crackers (For a wedding reception look for the heart shaped crackers available at Trader Joe's)		

Instructions:
Use kitchen scissors to cut the tomatoes in half or fourths. Soak them in plain or wine vinegar for at least one hour. Combine the remaining ingredients from olive oil through marjoram in a medium bowl. Drain tomatoes and add to herb - oil mixture and cover. (Save vinegar to use for salads). Let mixture stand at room temperature for 24 hours, stirring occasionally. Refrigerate (this mixture can be held in refrigerator for two weeks) Take out of refrigerator at least eight hours before party. Take cream cheese out of refrigerator at least four hours before event. Place cream cheese on

2 serving dishes with lip. Make deep X pattern over surface of cream cheese with a knife. Drain ½ of oil off of tomato mixture and then spoon remaining mixture evenly over the top of the cream cheese. Serve with crackers around the dish, or in separate basket.

Recipe Key   A
Storage Key   R
Schedule Key   5
Utensil Key   Spoon

Sweet and Sour Sausage Balls
60 – 80 Pieces

I made this recipe for the first time thirty-five years ago for my own engagement party. It has been taken to too many parties and functions to count. There are never any leftovers….If the pot is empty I have even seen people take meatballs from other dishes at potlucks and drop them into this sauce.

You can use lean bulk sausage (Jimmy Dean is preferred), make the meatballs and brown in the oven.
Or, omit the eggs and bread crumbs and use pre-browned link sausages. I recommend buying the 3lb bags in the freezer at Smart & Final. Cut each link into 3rds and drop in the sauce.

Amt	Item	Multiplied X	Total Quantity
4 lbs	Bulk Pork Sausage		
4 Ea	Eggs		
½ C	Bread crumbs – soft		
½ C	White wine vinegar		
¾ C	Brown Sugar		
3 C	Catsup – Please use the name brand catsup – it does make a difference		
½ C	Soy Sauce		

Instructions:
Mix sausage, eggs, and bread crumbs together. Shape into balls about the size of a walnut. You may bake in 350 deg oven until brown or, brown in frying pan until brown on all sides. Drain. Meatballs will finish cooking in sauce.

Combine catsup, soy sauce, brown sugar and vinegar in a large pan. Place meat balls in pan with sauce and simmer 30 minutes. Cool and then freeze. On the day of event warm thawed meatballs in sauce and place in crock pot or chafer to serve.

Notes: If using link sausages simmer for 30 minutes, put into container and freeze

Recipe Key	A
Storage Key	F
Schedule Key	1+
Utensil Key	Tongs

Tomato Cheese Bread
25 Pieces

Amt	Item	Multiplied X	Total Quantity
2 cubes	Softened butter		
4 Tbs	Olive oil		
½ C	Grated cheese (Parmesan, Cheddar or Jack or mix)		
½ C	Finely chopped oil-packed sun-dried tomatoes		
4Tbs	Chopped capers		
4 Ea	Large cloves garlic, minced		
	Dash of salt		
½ teas	Freshly ground pepper		
25 slices	French bread, sliced about 1 inch thick		

Instructions:

In a medium bowl beat together the butter and oil until smooth. Add the cheese, tomatoes, capers, garlic, salt and pepper and beat until blended. Spread on each slice of bread and place on a baking sheet. Broil 4-6 minutes and until bubbling and golden, then serve.

Notes: You can add more tomatoes and cheese to the amounts of butter and oil; also is great with homemade sun dried tomatoes. It is good with a few small salad shrimp placed on the top before broiling.

Recipe Key   A
Storage Key   R
Schedule Key   1
Utensil Key   Tongs

Cheese Tray with Fruit
24 Servings

Purchase an assortment from the following variety and then select two or three of the following to really pump up your cheese platter presentation. Use strawberries, kiwi fruit, or maybe a few of the small orange chilies that look like tiny pumpkins. If your function occurs in the fall, definitely plan on using figs. Purchase some type of large flat greens (grape leaves are wonderful but not readily available) to put under the fruit on one end of the tray. The fruit should be mounded (kiwi and figs can be cut length wise for visual appeal) and then cascade down one side of the tray.

Please purchase the best cheese you can afford. Unfortunately the large bricks of cheese sold at the "box stores" have high oil contents. Just the heat of a large group of people in a room can turn the cheese platter into an unappetizing glob of orange goop with puddles of oil. It is better to pay more, have less and have it eaten.

Our favorite store for cheese is Trader Joe's. They have different sized cuts so you can include a nice variety of cheese.

Cut into cubes or wedges, depending on the cheese, and put in a zip slide baggie.

Choose 2 - 2 1/2 lbs of the following

Amt	Item		Multiplied X	Total Quantity
	Brick	Gruyere		
	Brie	Havarti		
	Cheddar	Monterey Jack		
	Colby	Port du Salut		
	Edam	Stilton		
	Feta	Swiss		
	Gorgonzola			
	Gouda			
	Swiss			
2 lbs	Breton, Carr's or similar type cracker.			

Recipe Key   C
Storage Key   R
Schedule Key   3-4
Utensil Key   Tongs

Marinated Grilled Vegetables
30 Servings

We found these vegetables in a Grilled Pizza recipe….and love them all by themselves. They can be briefly seared on the grill outside and then finish cooking in the oven. The prep on this involves a little work; but a dish your guests will really appreciate because most of them wouldn't take the time to fix this themselves.

Amt	Item	Multiplied X	Total Quantity
2 C	Balsamic vinegar		
1 C	Olive oil (preferably extra-virgin)		
8 teas	Chopped fresh thyme		
4 teas	Grated lemon peel		
24	4-inch Portobello mushrooms, stemmed, gills cut out and discarded		
8	Large red bell peppers, halved, seeded		
8	Large yellow bell peppers, halved, seeded		
8	Large red onions cut into 1/2-inch-thick rounds		
Optional	Add any of the following and decrease the amount of peppers.		
2	Lbs medium sized carrots – cut in chunks. (use oven to finish cooking)		
6	Medium Zucchini squash – cut in 2" chunks		
6	Red Onions (cut in wedges – not rings.)		

Instructions:

Whisk vinegar, oil, thyme and lemon peel in large bowl to blend well. Add salt and pepper to taste. The vegetables can be placed in a baggie with the marinate for a few hours, or just brushed with the vinaigrette prior to going on the grill.

Prepare barbeque (medium-high heat). Brush vinaigrette over vegetables. Grill until mushrooms are tender and juicy, and peppers and onions are crisp-tender, about 12 minutes per side. To decrease the cooking time on the grill, increase the heat and just sear the veggies. Place on a cookie sheet in a 400 degree oven and bake until soft. Cut mushrooms and peppers into 1/2-inch-thick strips. Mix cooked veggies in a bowl. Add salt and pepper to taste. Serve at room temperature.

Recipe Key	A or V
Storage Key	R
Schedule Key	3-4
Utensil Key	Tongs

Vegetable Tray
24 Servings

Choose 3 lbs from the following

Amt	Item	Multiplied X	Total Quantity
	Asparagus spears		
	Broccoli florets		
	Baby Carrots		
	Cauliflower florets		
	Celery Sticks		
	Cherry tomatoes		
	Cucumber spears or circles		
	Green beans		
	Green Onions		
	Jicama		
	Mushrooms		
	Pea Pods		
	Radishes		
	Red, green or yellow peppers		
	Zucchini Spears		
1 QT Dip	Ranch is a favorite		

Instructions:
Clean all vegetables that you chose and place in separate zipped logged baggies. On the day of your event arrange on a tray around the dish you are using for the dip. We like to separate colors as much as possible. Cover with saran wrap and do not pour the dip until you are ready to set it out. We make a back up tray so it can be ready in a moments notice as needed.

Recipe Key	VT
Storage Key	R
Schedule Key	2-3
Utensil Key	Tongs, Small Spoon

Relish Tray
25 Servings

Choose 2 – 3 lbs Total

If you have a favorite relish item and this seems like too little, feel free to add more. There are times when relishes will really appeal to guests, and other times when they won't. A visually appealing tray of relishes should be heaping with a variety of colors and textures.

Amt	Item	Multiplied X	Total Quantity
	Black or green olives		
	Dill Spears		
	Pickled Beets		
	Pickled Eggs		
	Pickled Vegetables		
	Sweet Pickles		
	Marinated Artichoke Hearts		

Recipe Key   A or R
Storage Key   R
Schedule Key   2-3
Utensil Key   Tongs

Meat and Cheese Platter for Sandwiches
25 Servings

Select 5 lbs from the following meats

Select 3 lbs from the following cheeses - thinly sliced

Ham
Roast Beef
Swiss
Turkey
Pastrami
Corned Beef
Cold Cuts

American
Cheddar
Edam
Gouda
Monterey Jack
Munster
Provolone

Spreads/Other

Amt	Item	Multiplied X	Total Quantity
1/2 lb	Margarine or butter		
1 ½ C	Mayonnaise or salad dressing		
1 C	Mustard		
1 ½ lbs	Leaf Lettuce (optional)		
3 ½ lbs	Sliced Tomatoes (optional)		
35 ea	Small Buns or		
70 ea	Slices of bread		

Recipe Key   A/E
Storage Key   R
Schedule Key   2-3
Utensil Key   Tongs

Chicken and Mushroom Marsala
25 Servings

Amt	Item	Multiplied X	Total Quantity
13 Ea	Whole boneless chicken breasts with skin (about 8 lbs) halved		
6 ¼ Tbs	Olive oil		
14 ½ Tbs	Unsalted butter		
4 Ea	Onion, sliced thin		
3 lb	Mushrooms, sliced thin		
2 C	Marsala		
4 C	Chicken broth		
8 Tbs	Minced fresh parsley leaves		

Instructions:

Preheat oven to 350ºF. Mix all ingredients together and pour over chicken breasts. Bake until chicken is cooked through about 45 minutes.

We like to partially cook this dish, about ½ hour, and then finish cooking during the reheating stage. Refer to Food Handling Procedures if you do this. Cut each breast into 3 pieces prior to serving.

Notes: Can be warmed in a roaster or chafer prior to serving.

Recipe Key   E
Storage Key   R/F
Schedule Key   1+ or 2
Utensil Key   Slotted Spoon

Baked Chicken with Mushrooms and Artichokes
24 Servings

This is another tried and true recipe that appeals to everyone. It is simple to make but tastes very complicated. Serve with simple sides and you will get raves from your guests.

Amt	Item	Multiplied X	Total Quantity
12 ea	Boneless Chicken Breasts		
3 ea	6 oz jar marinated Artichoke Hearts		
24 ozs	Mushrooms, sliced		
2 ea	Bunches green onions, chopped…include ½ of green top part		
3 C	Dry White Wine		
1 ea	Bunch fresh Parsley		
2 ea	Lemon		
	Salt & Pepper		

Instructions:

This can be prepared in advance and reheated. Or, if you have oven space to cook at the site, it can be baking while the other foods are assembled. Simply combine all the ingredients to be placed on the chicken in baggies (see below). 1 ½ hours prior to serving put the chicken breasts in foil pans, cover with wine mixture & vegetables, add salt and pepper and pop in the oven.

Preheat oven to 350ºF. Season chicken breast halves with salt and pepper. Place skin side up in baking dish. Drain artichokes, reserving marinade. Cut artichokes in half. Place artichokes, mushrooms and green onions on top of chicken breasts. Combine reserved marinade (about 1 ½ Cups) and white wine and pour gently over chicken mixture. Bake until chicken is cooked through, about 45 minutes.

Chicken breasts should be sliced crosswise into three pieces prior to being put in chafing dish. Garnish chafer with fresh parsley and lemons quartered lengthwise.

Recipe Key	E
Storage Key	R
Schedule Key	3
Utensil Key	Tongs & Spoon

Rosemary Chicken

We haven't met anyone that doesn't like this dish.

The breasts can be prepped with yogurt and crumbs and then frozen. If you have enough oven room, plan on baking this dish while the prep work is being done. If not, partially cook, freeze and then finish cooking in the chafing dishes.

Amt	Item	Multiplied X	Total Quantity
12 breasts	8 lbs Boneless skinless chicken breasts		
3 1/3 C	Bread Crumbs (Unseasoned)		
1 2/3 C	Grated Parmesan Cheese		
6 ¼ C	Plain Yogurt		
3 ¾ tea	Powdered Dried Rosemary		
3 ¾ tea	Dried Thyme		
2 ½ tea	Garlic Powder		
2 ½ tea	Onion Powder		

Line baking sheet with tinfoil and spray with cooking spray

Cut each chicken breast in half.

Combine bread crumbs, Parmesan cheese, rosemary, thyme, onion powder and pepper in a plastic bag; shake until well mixed

Dip chicken in yogurt, place in plastic bag and shake until well coated. Arrange chicken in a single layer on baking sheet. After all chicken pieces have been coated with crumbs, sprinkle remaining crumbs over chicken pieces

At this point the chicken breasts can be covered lightly with saran and placed in the freezer.

After the breasts are frozen solid they can be placed in slide lock baggies.

Place on baking sheets and spray lightly with cooking spray.

Preheat oven to 400 degrees. Bake chicken 24 -35 minutes until golden brown and crisp. Cut each breast into three pieces prior to serving. If baking facilities are not available on the day of the function....cook about twenty minutes in oven....follow safe handling procedures to chill and then freeze.   Cut each breast in three pieces and place in chafers to finish cooking the day of the event.

Recipe Key   E
Storage Key   R/F
Schedule Key   1+
Utensil Key   Fork

Herb & Cream Cheese Stuffed Chicken Breasts
24 Servings

This is a recipe that we prepared for clients in the course of another business. Everyone loved this elegant cream cheese and herb stuffed chicken breast, so we decided to share our secret recipe with you.

The chicken breasts are assembled and then frozen. Pop in the oven 30 minutes before serving and listen to the raves!

Amt	Item	Multiplied X	Total Quantity
Cream Cheese Mixture			
¾ C	Butter – room temp		
24 oz	Cream Cheese		
6 Tea	Good Seasonings Dry Italian Dressing Mix		
6 TBL	Johnny's Dry Garlic Seasoning Mix		
Chicken	**Chicken Breasts**		
12 large	Skinless, boneless, fresh		
Egg Wash			
6 ea	Eggs		
1.5 C	Canned Evaporated Milk		
Bread Crumb Mixture			
3 – 4 Cups	Whole Wheat Bread Crumbs Make fresh or use packaged		
1 C	Parmesan Cheese		
1 C	Butter or margarine		
	Salt & Pepper		
	Cooking Spray		
	Toothpicks		

Blend all ingredients for the Cream Cheese mixture using a hand mixer. Cover and chill while the chicken is prepped.

Wash and pat chicken dry.

Lay waxed paper or saran on a flat surface.
Lay out a chicken breast
Cover with Saran
Use the flat side of a meat tenderizer to flatten the chicken breast to ¼ inch thickness.
Lightly salt and pepper the chicken breast

Make egg wash
Beat eggs in medium sized bowl and then add milk, continue beating until mixture is combined

Mix bread crumbs and grated cheese in a med sized bowl. Place a portion of the breadcrumb mixture in a pie pan – replenishing as needed

Spread cream cheese mixture in two strips down the length of the flattened chicken breast - leaving a 1 inch strip in the middle and ½ inch strips on each side and the ends bare.

Roll chicken breast tightly and secure with 2 toothpicks (the breast will be cut in half – the toothpick should be
In the middle of each piece after it is divided)

Set out small cookie sheets, or pie pans, that will fit in your freezer.

Dip each piece in the egg wash, roll in bread crumbs, pat the breast to make sure the crumbs adhere to the egg mixture and place on the cookie sheet.
After all the breasts are rolled, cover with saran and place the trays in the freezer for 2 hours.
Remove from the freezer and using a sharp knife, cut each piece of chicken in half. (each half will still be secured by a toothpick)
If the rolls are firmly frozen they may be gently layered in freezer bags (set on flat plate or other service to keep flat while assembling) If they are not firmly frozen cover with saran, return to freezer, and freeze until hard.
Once they are firmly frozen they may be layered in a freezer bag to conserve freezer space.

Remove the chicken breasts from the freezer the morning of the event. Place a single layer in shallow disposable pans that will go directly from the oven to the chafing dishes. The filling will ooze during baking and make it difficult to move the baked breasts from a cooking pan to the chafing dish.

Bake at 350 degrees for 30 to 40 minutes.

Recipe Key   E
Storage Key   F
Schedule Key   1+
Utensil Key   Tongs

Jambalaya
25 Servings

Amt	Item	Multiplied X	Total Quantity
4 Tbs	Butter		
4 Ea	Onions, chopped		
2 Ea	Bell peppers, chopped		
4 Ea	Bay leaves		
4 Ea	Garlic cloves, minced		
4 Ea	Sprigs fresh thyme or 1/2 teaspoon dried thyme		
½ teas	Ground cloves		
2 teas	Chili powder		
2 Ea	10-ounces can plum tomatoes		
4 C	Long-grain rice - Uncooked		
5 Qts	Chicken broth		
2 lb	Pickled pork or pork butt, diced (substitute smoked ham if pork is not available)		
2 lb	Sausage (cut into ½ inch slices) Can be any good smoked country sausage, kielbasa or venison sausage		
1 lb	Ham, diced		
1 ½ lb	Small shrimp		
2 Tbs	Louisiana or Cajun hot sauce (Can omit and have on table		
	Salt, pepper, and cayenne pepper to taste		

Instructions:

In a large heavy saucepan, melt butter and add diced pork, onions, peppers, bay leaves. Sauté until pork is browned and vegetables are soft. Add sausage and ham, sauté briefly. Add garlic, thyme, cloves, chili powder and tomatoes; cook for 5 minutes and then add rice and chicken stock. Bring to a boil, than reduce to a simmer for 15 minutes. Add shrimp, hot sauce and adjust seasoning, continue to cook until rice is done yet still firm.

Notes: Can be made ahead and frozen. Thaw and reheat in 350 degree oven for 45 minutes.

Recipe Key   E
Storage Key   R/F
Schedule Key   1+ or 2
Utensil Key   Spoon

Mojito Chicken

A wonderful Cuban recipe that draws raves whenever it is served. Making the marinade involves a process that will probably be new to you, but it does not take very long. The flavors released by the sweating process cannot be duplicated. All the compliments you will receive for this dish will make it worthwhile.

If possible we recommend baking the chicken while the other prep work is being done for the function. Of course, this depends on the oven situation. But, the meat cooks quickly and only needs to be cut into serving sized pieces before being placed on the buffet.
25 Servings

Amt	Item	Multiplied X	Total Quantity
	Marinade		
1/3 C	Chopped garlic		
¾ C	Chopped onion		
3 ¼ C	Fresh orange juice		
¾ C	Fresh lime juice		
¾ C	Olive oil		
6 teas	Kosher salt (I usually reduce the amount of salt considerably)		
1 ½ Tbs	Black pepper		
3 ¼ teas	Ground cumin		
3 ¼ teas	Dried oregano		
1 ½ Tbs	Chopped fresh cilantro		

Mix together the garlic, onion, orange juice, and lime juice in a bowl. Heat the olive oil in a large saucepan till just smoking. (Cover up your arms and put potholder mitts on your hands). Slide the contents of the bowl into the hot oil- be very careful because the liquid will splatter. (When I first prepared this dish the spattering was much less than I anticipated. However, please follow these precautions). Simmer for 5 minutes to soften the onions and garlic. Season the marinade with the rest of the ingredients. Pour everything into a blender or food processor and pulse 3 times to combine. Pour into a plastic container and cool to room temperature; then cover and refrigerate. Mojito Marinade keeps for up to two weeks.

Amt	Item	Multiplied X	Total Quantity
	Oven-Roasted Mojito Chicken		
9 lbs	Boneless Chicken Breasts		
4 Ea	Large onion, sliced into 1/2-inch rounds		
8 Tbs	Chopped fresh Italian parsley or cilantro		
	Mojito Marinade		

Instructions: Spread the chicken out in a baking dish, and pour the Mojito Marinade over it. Marinade for 4 hours or overnight in the refrigerator.

Heat oven to 375ºF. Scatter the onion slices over the bottom of a roasting pan and put the chicken on top, skin side up. Pour the remaining marinade over the chicken and bake for 1 hour and 15 minutes, until the chicken is golden and cooked through. Slice each breast into three pieces and arrange in the chafer; adding a bit of fresh Mojito Marinade to wake up the flavors. Spoon the onions and pan juices over the chicken. Sprinkle with parsley or cilantro and garnish with lime wedges.

Notes: Squeeze some lime over the portions for added flavor

Recipe Key   E
Storage Key   R/F
Schedule Key   5
Utensil Key   Fork

Penne with Roasted Tomatoes, Chicken, and Mushrooms
24 Servings

The roasted tomatoes combined with the feta cheese elevate this dish way above being a chicken and pasta entrée. A dish that is easy to prepare ahead of time and reheat in the oven.

Amt	Item	Multiplied X	Total Quantity
6 lbs	Roma tomatoes, quartered lengthwise, seeded, wedges halved		
1 C	Olive oil		
3 1/8 Tbs	Dried Oregano		
37 ½ oz	Penne pasta		
18 ¾ Ea	Small Portobello mushrooms, dark gills removed, caps sliced		
12 ½ Ea	Green onions, thinly sliced		
9 Ea	Garlic Cloves, minced		
2 1/3 lbs	Chicken tenders, halved lengthwise, then halved crosswise		
3 C	Crumbled feta cheese		
3 C	Grated Parmesan cheese		
1 ½ C	Low-salt chicken broth		
¾ C	Dry White wine		

Instructions:
Preheat oven to 425ºF. Combine tomatoes, 1 Tbs oil and oregano in small bowl, toss to blend. Place tomatoes on baking sheet, roast until beginning to dry and wrinkle-20 minutes.

Cook pasta in boiling water. Drain. Put the pasta in large bowls while you sauté the vegetables and chicken.

Use the pasta pan and heat 1-2 Tbs oil over medium high heat. Add mushrooms, onions and garlic – sauté until mushrooms are tender and brown – 10 minute. Transfer mushrooms to the bowl.

Salt & Pepper the chicken strips. Heat more oil in the pan and sauté chicken the batches until brown, about five minutes per batch. Heat another 1 Tbs of oil in pan over medium high heat. Add mushroom mixture and roasted tomatoes to pot. Add penne, chicken broth and wine, toss until heated through and sauce coats pasta. The cheese can be added directly to the dish, or served on the side.

Recipe Key   E
Storage Key   F/R
Schedule Key   3
Utensil Key   Fork/Spoon

Ham with Cola Lime Sauce

I have received a few marriage proposals at events where our clients served this sauce with a pre-cooked ham. If I had to choose our most popular recipe, this would be it!

If you purchase a spiral sliced ham at Costco, or Sam's Club, your meat entrée can't get any simpler. Simply cut the ham off the bone and put into slide lock baggies. A little of the sauce can be poured over the ham in the chafing dish; it can be set on the buffet to warm while the other prep work is being done. Your meal is ready.

Amt	Item	Multiplied X	Total Quantity
9-1/2 lb	Spiral Sliced Ham with bone		
	Lime Cola Sauce		
1 C	Coke Classic		
2 C	Packed dark or light brown sugar		
¼ C	Juice from 2 limes		
2 ea	Jalapeno chilies; cleaned + seeded, sliced crosswise into ¼ inch slices		

Bring Coke, lime juice, brown sugar and jalapenos to boil in a small saucepan over high heat. I remove the pepper slices after about 3 minutes. Reduce heat to medium-low and simmer until syrupy. Sauce can be made ahead of time and refrigerated.

Ham can be sliced off bone before hand and placed in slide lock baggies. Following the natural sectioning of the meat, make 3 or 4 cuts the length of the ham; cutting completely down to the bone. Gently remove sections and separate the spiral slices

Use the sauce to keep ham moist while it is being reheated in the oven or chafer. Do not overcook.

Recipe Key	E
Storage Key	F/R
Schedule Key	2
Utensil Key	Fork

Apricot and Habanero Glazed Pork Tenderloin

Amt	Item	Multiplied X	Total Quantity
4 ea	Small yellow onion, diced		
4 ea	Clove garlic, chopped		
4 ea	8 oz jar Apricot preserves		
4 ea	Habanero peppers, seeded and diced		
2 C	Orange Juice		
4 Tbs	Brown Sugar		
4 Tbs	Soy Sauce		
2 C	Water		
4 tea	Lime jest		
4 tea	Orange jest		
10 lb	Pork Tenderloin		
	Salt & Pepper		

Glaze

Sauté onion and garlic in oil until lightly colored. Add apricot preserves, habanero, orange juice, brown sugar, soy sauce and water. Cook approximately 20 minutes, until mixture thickens. Blend with hand mixer. Stir in lime zest and orange zest. Remove silver skin from pork tenderloins. Add salt and pepper. Brush with some of the apricot glaze.

Light grill and position rack approximately 6 inches above heat. Grill pork, brushing with more glaze often and turning frequently so the glaze does not burn. Cook 10 to 12 minutes, until internal temperature reaches 130 to 140 degrees F.

Place whole loin in freezer bags and freeze or, refrigerate for up to 3 days. Cut into medallions before serving.

Recipe Key   E
Storage Key   F/R
Schedule Key   1 + 3
Utensil Key   Fork

Claude's Famous BBQ Tri-Tip

You will see very few references to name brands in our recipes, but this is one of the exceptions. Words cannot describe what Claude's BBQ Brisket sauce does to tri-tip and brisket. There are no preservatives in the sauce; it gives the meat a very natural smoked flavor, but without overwhelming the taste of the meat. There won't be any left overs of any meat prepared with a Claude's sauce!
You can find Claude's sauces, and recipes, at www.claudessauces.com

24 Servings

Amt	Item	Multiplied X	Total Quantity
12 – 15 lbs	Beef Tri-tip		
2 ea	16 oz. bottle Claude's BBQ Brisket Sauce		

Marinate brisket in a plastic bag with Claude's BBQ Brisket sauce (2 ounces per pound of meat). Marinade in refrigerator overnight about 10 hours or longer.

Grill meat over medium heat until cooked to medium degree of doneness. Place tri-tips in baggies and freeze, or, refrigerate.

Reserve 2 cups of BBQ sauce and add 2 cups of water. On the day of the event the kitchen crew should prepare the meat by: slicing against the grain at an angle, placing in chafers or shallow pans, adding a small amount of reserved sauce to moisten meat, covering tightly with foil and re-heating on low heat in a 300 deg oven for 15 minutes. Meat may also be reheated directly in chafers if you are not serving large quantities.

Recipe Key	E
Storage Key	F/R
Schedule Key	1+
Utensil Key	Fork

Claude's Famous BBQ Brisket
24 Servings

You will see very few references to name brands in our recipes, but this is one of the exceptions. Words cannot describe what Claude's BBQ Brisket sauce does to tri-tip and brisket. There are no preservatives in the sauce; it gives the meat a very natural smoked flavor, but without overwhelming the taste of the meat. Any meat prepared with a Claude's sauces will be gone!

You can find Claude's sauces, and recipes, at www.claudessauces.com

Amt	Item	Multiplied X	Total Quantity
12 – 15 lbs	Beef Brisket		
2 ea	16 oz. bottle Claude's BBQ Brisket Sauce		

Marinate brisket in a plastic bag with Claude's BBQ Brisket sauce (2 ounces per pound of meat). Marinade in refrigerator overnight about 10 hours or longer. Place brisket in a roaster pan with the fat side up, and pour the sauce over it. Seal pan with foil or with tight lid. Cook in slow oven at 300 for 45 minutes per pound, about 6 hours. Remove from oven, cool, and cut off fat. The sauce can be used as a natural gravy, remove fat from sauce by cooling in refrigerator, fat will float to top and can be taken out easily.

Cut into pieces just small enough to fit into freezer bags and place in the freezer.

Reserve 2 cups of BBQ sauce and add 2 cups of water. On the day of the event the kitchen crew should prepare the meat by: slicing against the grain at an angle, placing in chafers or shallow pans, adding a small amount of reserved sauce to moisten meat, covering tightly with foil and re-heating on low heat in a 300 deg oven for 15 minutes. Meat may also be reheated directly in chafers if you are not serving large quantities. The brisket can also be served for sandwiches.

Recipe Key   E
Storage Key   F/R
Schedule Key   1+
Utensil Key   Fork

Smoked Pork Shoulder

One of the most economical cuts of meat you can find at the supermarket. But, another one of those dishes that people will rave about. If you want left-overs, purchase and cook an extra piece of meat; as there won't be a shred of meat left at your function.

In the meat case at the store, this looks just like a ham that has not been cured. This is prepared on a Charcoal or Gas Grill; with a lid

Amt	Item	Multiplied X	Total Quantity
10-12 lb	Raw Ham Shoulder		
1 bag	Hickory Chips or Chunks		
2	Bottles of your favorite BBQ sauce		
4	Shallow aluminum drip pans for the BBQ		
1 or 2	Empty aluminum cans (Large tuna cans work the best)		
	Heavy Duty Aluminum Foil & an extra large spring type office clip		

Lightly salt and pepper meat

To prepare to smoke the shoulder
   1)   Soak the wood chips for at least ½ hour covered with water.
   2a) To cook using a Charcoal grill

   Remove grill and prepare the BBQ; starting the briquettes about 1 hour prior to cooking. When coals are hot, distribute evenly around the outer rim of the BBQ. Place aluminum drip tray in the center. Put the grill in place. Add 2 cups water to the drip pan and place the meat on the grill. Pack the water soaked wood chips in the empty aluminum can and place next to the meat. Cover. Add additional briquettes every hour to maintain medium heat in the BBQ

   2b) To cook using a gas grill

   Remove the grill and 1/3 of the lava rock. Move all the remaining rocks to one side of the grill. Preheat the rocks for 15 minutes. Place aluminum drip tray opposite the lava rocks. Put the grill in place. Add 2 cups water to the drip pan and place the meat on the grill. Pack the water soaked wood chips in the empty aluminum can and place on the grill over the hot rocks. Cover.

You can cook two roasts at one time, using this method. Just rotate and/ or turn the roast over every forty five minutes.

To decrease the cooking time; cover all the open ports on the gas grill. This can be accomplished by cutting a piece of tin foil long enough to go completely around the BBQ, at the handle section, with 4 inches extra. After cutting the piece of foil, fold the *lengthwise* outer edges to meet in the middle, and then fold in half *lengthwise* again. This will give you a sturdy piece of foil about 4 – 6 inches wide. Hold one end in front, wrap the foil around the side toward the back (to cover the hole for the rotisserie) across the rear, around the side toward the front (to cover the opposite rotisserie opening) and finally across the front to meet with the start of the piece of foil. Secure the ends together with an extra large office clip or clamp.

Because the heat source is on one side of the grill, plan on rotating the meat every 45 minutes. You can cook two roasts, placed on the "cold" side of the grill, at one time, using this method. Just rotate and/or turn the roast over every forty five minutes. You will be able to determine which side needs exposure during the cooking process by the observing the color and texture of the meat.

The water will evaporate over a period of time. Add additional water as needed to keep the grease from popping.

Replace the wood chips when after they turn black.

Use a meat thermometer to determine when the meat is done. The average cooking time for two roasts on a gas grill is four hour to five hours.

After meat is fully cooked, remove from grill and let stand to cool. When the meat is cool enough to handle cut off fat layer and cut or shred the meat. Place in large slide lock baggies and either freeze or refrigerate.

Serve the BBQ sauce in a bowl as an accompaniment to the meat on the buffet. Serving large dinner rolls will enable guests to make a manageable sized sandwich if they desire.

Recipe Key	E
Storage Key	F/R
Schedule Key	1+
Utensil Key	Fork

Ham and Egg Strata

The 2nd best thing about this dish is that you prepare it a day ahead of time. But, the best thing is the great taste!

Serves 24

Amt	Item	Multiplied X	Total Quantity
16 2/3 C	Milk (do not use low-fat or nonfat)		
33 Ea	Large eggs		
2 Tab 2 1/3 tea	Dry Mustard		
2 Tab 2 1/3 tea	Salt		
	Large eggs		
33 Ea	Slices white sandwich bread, crusts trimmed, cut into 1 inch pieces		
8 1/3 C	Diced ham		
4 Ea	Green bell pepper, chopped (optional)		
2 C	Chopped onion		
4 C	Packed grated sharp cheddar cheese		

Instructions:

Butter 4 ea 12 x 9 x 2-inch glass baking dish. Beat milk, eggs, mustard and salt in large bowl to blend. Mix in bread, ham, green pepper and onion. Transfer mixture to prepared dish. Cover and chill overnight. Or use larger disposable baking pans and adjust cooking time accordingly to 1 hour 15 minutes to 1 hour 30 minutes.

Preheat over to 375ºF. Bake strata uncovered until just set in center, about 50 minutes. Sprinkle cheese over. Bake until cheese melts, about 5 minutes longer. Let stand 10 minutes and then cut into squares to serve.

Recipe Key   E
Storage Key   R
Schedule Key   1
Utensil Key   Spoon

Egg Cheese & Sausage Strata
24 Servings

Amt	Item	Multiplied X	Total Quantity
6C	Milk (do not use low fat or non-fat)		
21 ea	Large eggs		
2 tea	Dry Mustard		
1lb 4oz	Slices white bread, cut into 1 inch cubes		
4.5 lbs	Bulk Sausage (Jimmy Dean is recommended)		
2 C	Chopped Onion		
1 lb 4 oz	Grated Sharp cheddar cheese		
	Salt & Pepper		

Brown the sausage in a frying pan over med high heat in batches until the meat is no longer pink and then drain off any excess fat. While sausage is browning, grease a 12x20x2 inch baking pan. Or use several smaller pans. If Strata will be served in chafing dishes use disposable ½ hotel pans….two will fit perfectly into each chafer. Place bread cubes in pan and layer the sausage and then the cheese on top of the cubes. Combine eggs, milk and mustard. Pour over mixture in pans, distributing as evenly as possible. Refrigerate overnight.

Bake at 325 uncovered approximately one hour, or until set.

Let rest 10 minutes, cut into squares to serve

Recipe Key   E
Storage Key   R
Schedule Key   1
Utensil Key   Spoon

Vegetarian Jambalaya
24 Servings

This is a modification of our Jambalaya recipe that your vegetarian guests will love. The addition of black beans provides protein so you have all the bases covered.

Amt	Item	Multiplied X	Total Quantity
4 Tbs	Butter		
4 Ea	Onions, chopped		
2 Ea	Bell peppers, chopped		
4 Ea	Bay leaves		
4 Ea	Garlic cloves, minced		
4 Ea	Sprigs fresh thyme or 1/2 teaspoon dried thyme		
½ teas	Ground cloves		
2 teas	Chili powder		
2 Ea	10-ounces can plum tomatoes		
4 C	Long-grain rice - Uncooked		
5 Qts	Vegetable broth		
6 Ea	15 oz cans black beans (can be seasoned, etc if not meat)		
2 Tbs	Louisiana or Cajun hot sauce (Can omit and have on table		
	Salt, pepper, and cayenne pepper to taste		

Instructions:
In a large heavy saucepan, melt butter and add onions, peppers, bay leaves. Sauté until vegetables are soft. Add garlic, thyme, cloves, chili powder and tomatoes; cook for 5 minutes and then add rice and beans and vegetable stock. Bring to a boil, then reduce to a simmer until rice is done yet still firm.
Notes: This can be made ahead and frozen.

Recipe Key	E
Storage Key	R/F
Schedule Key	1+ or 2
Utensil Key	Spoon

Pecan Crusted Chicken Salad

This is another recipe from a famous restaurant that everyone loves. The chicken and dressing are prepped and baked in advance and then assembled the day of the event.

24 Servings

Amt	Item	Multiplied X	Total Quantity
	Chicken		
6 lbs	Boneless skinless chicken breasts		
12 C	Chopped Pecans (we bought in bulk food section for considerable savings)		
8 C	Flour		
12 Ea	Eggs		
2 - 3 oz	Milk		
	Vegetable oil		
	Glazed Pecans		
1.5 C	Dark Brown Sugar		
6 T	Water		
	Salad		
12	Heads of Romaine Lettuce (or bags of chopped romaine)		
1.5 C	Balsamic Vinaigrette Salad Dressing (We used Ken's Steakhouse brand)		
6 Small Cans	Mandarin Oranges		
3 C	Craisins		
16 oz	Bleu cheese crumbles		

Preheat oven to 350 deg

Combine **6 C pecans** and **4 C flour** in food processor; pulse until nuts are finely chopped.

Mix eggs and milk for batter

Place **remaining 4 C flour** in one bowl, egg batter in second bowl and pecan flour in third bowl.

Flatten chicken breasts with a meat tenderizer between sheets of saran to 1/4 inch thick.

Coat chicken in plain flour, then in egg batter and third in pecan flour.

Heat oil in heavy skillet over medium heat

Sauté chicken breasts in batches until just browned on both sides. Let pan recover back to medium heat between batches if necessary.

Bake chicken breasts for 7 to 8 minutes until fully cooked (160 degrees internal temp), cool completely and then place on cookie sheet or pie pans, cover lightly with saran and freeze just long enough to set the pecan coating. Place frozen breasts in freezer bags and freeze until the day of the event.

Glazed Pecans – Mix remaining pecans with brown sugar and water and heat until sugar syrup is clear. Set aside to cool. When thoroughly cooled off place in air tight container. If pecan mixture is made more than a week ahead it can be refrigerated or frozen. If it is made several days prior to the event it can be stored at room temperature.

Salad assembly
Craisins and blue cheese crumbles
Drain mandarin oranges
Cut chicken breasts into large bite sized pieces
Layer romaine, oranges, Craisins, blue cheese crumbles, glazed pecans and chicken pieces in large salad bowls.
Dress lightly with vinaigrette and toss.

Recipe Key	S
Storage Key	F/R
Schedule Key	4
Utensil Key	Salad Servers

Artichoke Rice Salad
24 Servings

Another recipe shared with us by a client. This is a very distinctive dish with a wonderful combination of flavors.

Amt	Item	Multiplied X	Total Quantity
4 Pkgs	Lipton's Onion Soup Mix		
6 ¼ C	Uncooked Long Grain Rice		
12	Green Onions, sliced		
2	Green peppers diced		
34	Stuffed Green Olives		
8	6 oz jars Marinated Artichoke hearts		
1 tea	Curry Powder (or more to taste)		
1 1/3 C	Mayonnaise		

Instructions:
Cook rice as directed. Drain artichokes, reserving marinade and slice. Combine marinade with curry and mayonnaise. Add rest of ingredients and stir in dressing. Mix well and refrigerate.

Notes: You can cook rice in advance and freezing it. Then have the artichokes and green olives chopped and ready to go in a separate container. Mix with freshly cut green onions the day before or day of serving. If you do not care for green peppers, leave them out and add more green olives for the color.

Recipe Key   S
Storage Key   F/R
Schedule Key   4
Utensil Key   Spoon

Broccoli Salad
24 – 30 Servings

If you like Broccoli salad this will knock your socks off. It makes the deli salad pale by comparison.

Amt	Item	Multiplied X	Total Quantity
5 Heads	Broccoli		
3 /13 ea	Medium Red Onions		
3 ½ C	Sunflower Seeds		
1 2/3 C	Raisins		
1 ½ lb	Bacon (cut into small pieces w/scissors, cook thoroughly, place on paper towel to absorb grease)		
3 ½ C	Mayonnaise		
¾ C	Sugar		
2 ¼ Tbs	Vinegar		

Instructions:
Break broccoli into small flowerets. Add onions, raisins, sunflower seeds and bacon. Mix together mayo, sugar and vinegar, pour over salad, and toss.

Place in slide lock baggies to store; they will take up less refrigerator space than a large bowl.

Best if made ahead so the flavors have time to combine and mellow.

Recipe Key   S
Storage Key   R
Schedule Key   3
Utensil Key   Spoon

Greek Salad
24 – 30 Servings

This recipe was given to us by a distant relative of Zorba. Well, not exactly. But he sure looked like him!

This salad is visually stunning and is a wonderful addition to a summertime buffet when vine ripened tomatoes are available at your local farmer's market. Our favorite cost saving ploy is to show up late and barter with the vendors. They will usually prefer to drop the price, rather than drag everything back to the farm.

Amt	Item	Multiplied X	Total Quantity
3 ¼ lb	Tomatoes, seeded and diced (about 9 cups)		
8 ¾ C	Cucumbers, peeled and chopped		
4 C	Diced Red Peppers		
1 ¼ C	Pitted Kalamata Olives or other brine cured black olives – halved		
1 ¼ C	Diced Red Onion		
¾ C	Chopped fresh Italian (flat leaf) parsley		
¾ C	Extra Virgin Olive Oil		
¼ C + 1 Tbs	Red Wine Vinegar		
2 tea	Dried Oregano		
1 C	Crumbled Feta Cheese		

Instructions:
Bag all above ingredients into slide lock bags to be combined on day of event.
Toss first 9 ingredients in medium bowl to blend. Gently mix in cheese. Season with salt and pepper. (Can be combined 2 hours ahead. Let stand at room temperature.)
Recipe Key   S
Storage Key   R
Schedule Key   2
Utensil Key   Spoon

Greek-Italian Chopped Salad
24 Servings

This salad is a nice alternative to the standard Caesar salad.

Amt	Item	Multiplied X	Total Quantity
1 ½ C	Olive Oil		
¾ C	Red Wine Vinegar		
1 ½ Tbs	Dried Oregano		
5 ea	Small garlic cloves, minced		
3 ea	15 ½ oz cans garbanzo beans (chickpeas) drained and rinsed		
3 ea	Red Bell peppers, diced		
3 C	Very thinly sliced red onions		
3 C	Very thinly sliced fresh fennel bulb		
1 C	Crumbled Feta Cheese (about 12.5 oz)		
¾ C	Sliced pitted Kalamata Olives		
12 C	Chopped Romaine lettuce		

Instructions

Whisk oil, vinegar oregano, and garlic in small bowl to blend. Season the dressing to taste with salt and pepper. This can be made 2 to three days prior to event. Store the dressing in a container or slide lock bag.

Dice, slice and cut all other ingredients except romaine lettuce two days prior to event

Store into slide lock bags, and mark for salad so nothing is missed.

Notes: Romaine can be cut same day of event.

Recipe Key   S
Storage Key   R
Schedule Key   2
Utensil Key   Salad Servers

Oh So Easy Pasta Salad
24 Servings

This salad is colorful, has a nice zip and is easy to make.
It has a variety of textures and flavors, and is an economical way to feed a crowd.

Amt	Item	Multiplied X	Total Quantity
1 lb 4oz	Uncooked tri colored pasta		
1	Bottle Cheese Italian Dressing		
3 ea	1lb Packages Frozen Broccoli, Cauliflower & Carrot Combination		
2 ea	Small cans Diced Black Olives		
2 C	Grated Parmesan Cheese		

Directions:
Cook pasta in two batches using a large pot and at least one gall of boiling water. Or cook at one time in two pans. Place half of frozen vegetables in colander while pasta cooks. After the pasta is cooked, slightly past a la dente; about 12 minutes, pour the pasta and water on top of vegetables in the colander. The hot water will "cook" the veggies perfectly. Repeat for the additional pasta and veggies. Pour the pasta and veggies into a large bowl. Drain the diced black olives and add to the bowl. Add salad dressing until pasta is covered with oil mixture. Salt and Pepper to taste. Place in slide lock baggies and refrigerate. Add more dressing (the pasta will absorb the initial dressing) and the cheese just prior to serving.

Recipe Key	S
Storage Key	R
Schedule Key	3
Utensil Key	Spoon

My Sons' Favorite Potato Salad
24 Servings

Amt	Item	Multiplied X	Total Quantity
6 lbs	New Potatoes		
6 ea	Hard Cooked Eggs		
2 C	Diced Onion		
2 C	Diced Celery		
1 C	Minced Sweet Pickles, reserve juice		
3 C	Miracle Whip Salad Dressing		
3 Tbs	Prepared Mustard		
4 Tea	Spice Island Beau Monte Seasoning		
	Salt & Pepper		

Wash potatoes and cut into large bite sized pieces. Cook the potatoes in two pans or two batches. Place ½ of potatoes in large pan and fill 2/3 full of water. Lightly salt. Cover and cook on high heat until potatoes are fork tender. Do no overcook. Place eggs in a pan of cold water and bring to a rolling boil. Boil for 12 minutes. Drain hot water out of egg pan. Bounce the eggs in the pan to break the shell. Run cold water in pan for a minute or two until heat has dissipated. Cover eggs with cold water and set aside to cool.

After potatoes are cooked, drain off all water and cool to room temperature. To make dressing for salad; mix mustard, Miracle Whip and Beau Monde Seasoning together in a medium sized bowl, add about two tablespoons of the sweet pickle juice. Add salt and pepper to taste. Peel and chop hard boiled eggs. Place potatoes, onion, celery, sweet pickles and eggs in a very large bowl. Or, two large bowls. Add dressing and mix all ingredients together. Cover and refrigerate for several hours. Taste test to determine if additional salt and pepper, or Miracle Whip, needs to be added. Sometimes the potatoes absorb more dressing than anticipated. If the salad seems dry add the Miracle whip straight from the jar and mix well. Adjust salt and pepper.

Recipe Key	S
Storage Key	R
Schedule Key	2
Utensil Key	Spoon

Simple Potato Salad
Simple because it relies on real mayonnaise for it's wonderful flavor

Amt	Item	Multiplied X	Total Quantity
6 lbs	New Potatoes		
6 ea	Hard Cooked Eggs		
2 C	Diced Red Onion		
2 C	Diced Celery		
3 C	Best Food Mayonnaise		
2 ea	Diced Green Peppers (Optional		

Wash potatoes and cut into large bite sized pieces. Cook the potatoes in two pans or two batches. Place ½ of potatoes in large pan and fill 2/3 full of water. Lightly salt. Cover and cook on high heat until potatoes are fork tender. Do no overcook. Place eggs in a pan of cold water and bring to a rolling boil. Boil for 12 minutes. Drain hot water out of egg pan. Bounce the eggs in the pan to break the shell. Run cold water in pan for a minute or two until heat has dissipated. Cover eggs with cold water and set aside to cool.

After potatoes are cooked, drain off all water and cool to room temperature. Peel and chop the hard boiled eggs. Place potatoes, onion, celery, and eggs in a very large bowl. Or, two large bowls. Add Mayonnaise, salt and pepper and mix all ingredients together. Cover and refrigerate for several hours. Taste test to determine if additional salt and pepper, or mayonnaise needs to be added. Sometimes the potatoes absorb more dressing than anticipated. If the salad seems dry, keep adding a few tablespoons of the mayonnaise and mix well until the desired consistency is obtained. Adjust salt and pepper.

Recipe Key   S
Storage Key   R
Schedule Key   2
Utensil Key   Spoon

Pasta & Shrimp Salad
Serves 24

A light refreshing salad.

Amt	Item	Multiplied X	Total Quantity
12 oz	Uncooked Radiatore Pasta (Frilly shaped pasta, short thick and compact)		
¼ C	Chopped green onions		
10 oz	Snow peas, thawed and uncooked		
1 lb	Small Shelled Cooked Shrimp		
	Lemon Basil Dressing		
1 C	Cider Vinegar		
¾ C	Lemon juice		
3 oz	Granulated sugar 1/4 C + 3 Tbsp		
1 ½ Tbsp	Salt		
2 ¼ Tbsp	Dried basil		
1 ½ C	Salad oil		

Combine Vinegar, lemon juice, sugar, salt, and dried basil leaves. Gradually add salad oil. Mix well, store in refrigerator.

Cook pasta until tender. Drain. Yield should be approximately 1.5 lbs pasta. Add dressing and toss to coat. Chill. Add onions, snow peas and shrimp just before serving.

Recipe Key	S
Storage Key	R
Schedule Key	2
Utensil Key	Spoon

The Best Spinach Salad
24 Servings

Amt	Item	Multiplied X	Total Quantity
1 C	Vegetable Oil		
1/2	Onion, (Vidalia or other sweet variety preferred) finely diced		
4 Tbs	Brown Sugar – packed		
½ C	Red Wine Vinegar		
4 Tbs	Catsup		
2 tea	Worcestershire Sauce		
2 tea	Dry or French style Mustard		
2 lbs	Baby Spinach, washed and drained		
12 ea	Mushrooms sliced		
4 ea	Hard Boiled Eggs, chopped		
½	Red Onion – thinly sliced		
½ C	Dried Cranberries (Optional)		
8	Slices Bacon, Fried and Crumbled		

Combine first eight ingredients in a blender, pulse to mix ingredients, and add salt and pepper to taste. Place in container with a tight lid and refrigerate. Clean and slice mushrooms, peel eggs, slice the red onion and place in slide lock baggies. On the day of the function; combine all salad ingredients just before serving and add dressing. Toss lightly.

Recipe Key   S
Storage Key   R
Schedule Key   2-3
Utensil Key   Salad Server

Simple Green Salad
24 Servings

The fastest way to bring a buffet line to a dead halt is to have several different salad dressings for your guests to choose from. We believe in making life easy …have the salad dressed in the kitchen with a good bottled vinaigrette dressing and everyone will be happy. We recommend that Ranch dressing be used as a dip for the fresh veggies. It is heavy and hard to work with when a salad is being pre-dressed.
Again, you can't beat Costco for produce.
Buy a few bags of the Spring Mix lettuce, a big bag or two of the head lettuce and a bag of romaine hearts if your guest count is climbing. Add croutons, throw in cherry tomatoes for garnish and the salad is ready.

Amt	Item	Multiplied X	Total Quantity
3.5 lbs	Iceberg Lettuce		
3.5 lbs	Leaf, Bib, Romaine or Spring Mix Lettuce		
3 C	Bottled Balsamic Vinaigrette		
2 boxes	Garlic Croutons		
2 boxes	Cherry or Grape Tomatoes		

Pre-wash lettuce and place in the giant slide lock baggies. If using romaine, tear the lettuce into bite sized pieces. Take from refrigerator and place all the items in paper grocery bags to be transported to the site together. Mark the outside of the bag with a magic marker: SALAD

Recipe Key	S
Storage Key	R
Schedule Key	2-3
Utensil Key	Salad Server

Caesar Salad

Use the same portions as for Simple Green salad but use all romaine and substitute a good Caesar dressing.

Amt	Item	Multiplied X	Total Quantity
7 lbs	Romaine Lettuce		
3 C	Caesar Dressing		
2 Boxes	Croutons		

Rinse Romaine heads and let dry. Tear romaine into bit sized pieces and put in large plastic slide lock bags.

Salad should be dressed just prior to serving.

Recipe Key	S
Storage Key	R
Schedule Key	2-3
Utensil Key	Salad Server

Ambrosia
24 Servings

This is another salad that people really enjoy, but don't take the time to make at home so it is usually a big hit. Serve it in addition to fresh fruit on a brunch buffet.

Amt	Item	Multiplied X	Total Quantity
24 oz	Canned Mandarin Oranges, drained		
32 oz	Canned Pineapple Tidbits, drained		
6 oz	Miniature Marshmallows		
3 oz	Shredded Coconut		
6 oz	Sour Cream		

Combine fruit, marshmallows and coconut. Place in slide lock baggies and refrigerate. Add sour cream just prior to serving. Toss lightly to combine.

Recipe Key	S
Storage Key	R
Schedule Key	1-2
Utensil Key	Spoon

Velvet Chicken Salad
25 Servings

Amt	Item	Multiplied X	Total Quantity
13 – 14 lbs	Un-cooked whole chicken or 6 lbs uncooked boneless chicken breasts		
3 lbs	Minced Celery		
¼ C	Finely Minced Onions		
2 lbs	Red or Green Grapes cut in half		
1 1/2 C	Mayonnaise		
1 C	Sour Cream		
4 TBS	Red Raspberry Vinegar		
	Salt & Pepper		
25-30	Rolls or Mini-Croissants		

Instructions

Stew whole chickens by placing in large pot, cover with water, sprinkle with salt & pepper. Cover and cook approximately 45 minutes to 1 hour over med to low heat. Remove from water and cool enough that bird can be skinned and meat removed from the bones. Chop meat into cubes the size of a walnut or less. Freeze the stock for future use if desired.

If using whole boneless chicken breasts, place in large shallow pan in one layer. Add ½ Cup water, sprinkle with salt and pepper, cover pan tightly with foil. Bake in 325 degree oven until breasts are done; 30 – 45 minutes. Remove from oven. As soon as the meat is cool enough to handle, cut each breast lengthwise into strips and then crosswise into pieces the size of a walnut or smaller. Place meat in container, cover loosely and place in refrigerator to cool. Meat may be cooked in advance and frozen. Combine with other ingredients a day prior to serving.

Combine all ingredients. If wetter mixture is desired, additional mayo or sour cream may be added. Add more vinegar to taste….it will give a slight sweet taste of raspberry to the salad. Add salt and pepper to taste. You may pre-assemble sandwiches on mini-croissants, or place mixture next to a basket of bread or rolls and have guests assemble their own sandwich.

Recipe Key   A
Storage Key   F/ R
Schedule Key   2
Utensil Key   Spoon

Drunken Rice
24 Servings

One of our clients shared this recipe with us. It has proven to be a great alternative to regular rice or pilaf. The addition of the mushrooms, onions and garlic, not to mention the subtle flavor picked up from cooking the rice with a little wine, makes this a real stand alone dish. You won't need any additional butter or sauce to serve with it.

Amt	Item	Multiplied X	Total Quantity
3	Medium onions, finely chopped		
6	Cloves garlic, minced		
1 ½ C	Butter		
7 1/3 Tbs	Parsley, finely chopped		
¾ tea	Marjoram		
¾ tea	Thyme		
3 ¼ C	Long Grain white rice, uncooked		
4 ¾ C	Chicken broth or vegetable stock		
1 ½ C	Dry white wine or water		
3 lbs	Fresh mushrooms, sliced		
1/3 C	Lemon Juice		
1 ½ C	Parmigiano Reggiano or Romano cheese, freshly grated.		

Instructions:

Cook rice separately with broth and wine. Our favorite way to cook rice is to put the rice and liquid in a pan with a tight fitting lid. Turn burner on high, when liquid comes to boil set timer for 1 minute. After 1 minute is up, reduce heat to low and set timer for 5 minutes. After 5 minutes, turn off the heat but leave the pan tightly covered on the burner.

Do not peek. After 25 minutes you will have perfectly cooked rice. We live in a high altitude and this even works perfectly for us.

In a 3 quart casserole with a lid, combine onion, garlic and butter, microwave on high for 3 minutes. Mix in parsley, marjoram, thyme, lemon juice and mushrooms. Microwave covered for 3-4 minutes. Add to rice, fluff and serve with cheese.

Notes: Rice can be cooked ahead and frozen. Reheat and mix with other ingredients on day of event.

Recipe Key	R/P
Storage Key	F/R
Schedule Key	5
Utensil Key	Spoon

Baked Red Potatoes with Sautéed Peppers and Cheese
24 Servings

Pre-boil the potatoes and sauté the peppers ahead of time.
Assemble with the grated cheese at the site of your function and pop in the oven.
If an oven is not available, have a helper bake in the morning and then re-heat in chafers.

Amt	Item	Multiplied X	Total Quantity
8 lbs	Red Skinned Potatoes		
2 ea	Green Peppers, cleaned and cut in lengthwise strips as wide as your finger		
2 ea	Red Peppers, cleaned and cut in lengthwise strips as wide as your finger		
3 ea	Red Onions, cleaned and cut in lengthwise strips as wide as your finger		
2 C	Butter		
1 ½ lb	Grated Cheddar Cheese		

Rinse potatoes and cut into 4 to 6 pieces each. Cook in batches, depending on the size of your pot. Cover 2/3 of potatoes with water, add sprinkle of salt and cover tightly. Cook on med high heat until potatoes are fork tender. While potatoes are cooking, melt part of butter in a large skillet and add enough vegetables to completely cover the bottom of the skillet. Sauté the peppers and onions until limp and fork tender. You will probably need to cook in two to three batches. Cool sautéed vegetables, put in slide lock baggies; with the butter they were cooked in, and then refrigerate. When potatoes are done, drain off all water. Place in open container to partially cool. When potatoes have completely cooled place in slide lock baggie and refrigerate.

Spray baking pans with Pam. To assemble; layer potatoes, peppers, onions and cheese in disposable ½ size hotel pan or put directly into hotel pan for chafer.

Place in 350 degree oven, uncovered, until potatoes are hot and cheese melts; about 20 minutes.

Recipe Key   R/P
Storage Key   R
Schedule Key   3
Utensil Key   Spoon

Mashed Potatoes with Fontina Cheese and Italian Parsley
24 Servings

No, these are not low fat mashed potatoes. But, the combination of half and half with the fontina cheese gives these potatoes a surprisingly different flavor.

Amt	Item	Multiplied X	Total Quantity
8 ½ lbs	Medium-size russet potatoes, or substitute red skinned potatoes - but do not peel		
3 ¼ C	Half and half		
1 Stick	Butter		
1 ½ lbs	Packed grated Fontina Cheese		
1 ½ C	Chopped fresh Italian parsley		

Instructions:
Peel russets and cut in half length wise. Then cut each of those halves into thirds. Or, scrub reds and cut in half and then cut each half in half again.
Cook in batches by putting approximately 2 inches of hot water in the bottom of the pan, adding potatoes to within two inches of top of pan, sprinkle with salt, cover with a tight fitting lid and steam until potatoes are folk tender. Monitor water level during cooking.
When potatoes are done, drain off remaining water.
Thoroughly mash potatoes and then add begin adding half and half. Add butter, stir vigorously until butter melts and potatoes are smooth. Stir into 2/3 of cheese and ¾ cup parsley. Add salt and pepper to taste. Transfer potatoes into baking dish. Potatoes can be refrigerated at this point if they are going to be reheated at the time of the event.

To serve:
Sprinkle with remaining cheese and parsley.
Preheat oven to 425ºF. Bake potatoes until heated through and cheese melts, about 15 minutes. If potatoes will be served in a chafing dish, the initial pans of potatoes can be heated in the chafers if the oven is too small to hold all the pans.

Recipe Key	R/P
Storage Key	R
Schedule Key	5
Utensil Key	Spoon

Brown & Wild Rice with Cranberries and Pine-nuts
24 Servings

Another recipe shared with us by a dear friend. This is a refreshing combination of rice, orange juice, cranberries and pine-nuts. This dish is very satisfying, but not too heavy. Best of all, it needs no additional sauce and can be served hot, cold, or at room temperature.

Amt	Item	Multiplied X	Total Quantity
1.5 Lbs	Brown, White and Wild Rice (uncooked)		
2	Onions diced		
4 Tbs	Grated Orange Rind		
¾ C	Orange juice to moisten		
1/3 C	Fresh Parsley		
1 ¼ C	Dried Cranberries		
¾ C	Toasted Pine-nuts		
	Olive Oil		

Instructions

Cook rice with diced onions until the rice is tender. Add grated orange rind and enough orange juice to moisten rice. Then add the parsley, dried cranberries and toasted pine-nuts. Add salt & pepper to taste.

Add a small amount of olive oil and mix well. You should be able to detect a very slight sheen on the rice from the oil.
Place in a 350 deg oven for 45 minutes.
Cool. Place in zip slide bags and freeze or refrigerate.
If serving in a chafing dish, spray with Pam to make clean up easier.

Recipe Key   R/P
Storage Key   R/F
Schedule Key   1 + 4
Utensil Key   Spoon

Herbed Red Potatoes
24 Servings

Amt	Item	Multiplied X	Total Quantity
35 Ea	Small new potatoes		
8 1/3 Tbs	Butter		
8 1/3 teas	Minced fresh parsley		
8 1/3 teas	Minced fresh chives		

Instructions:

Peal strip around center of potato and place in cold water. Add water to cover all potatoes and bring to a boil. Cook until done. Drain any remaining water from potatoes. Sauté butter, parsley and chives in pan, toss with potatoes and keep warm

Notes: Can be cooked the day before and reheated in roaster or chafer.

Recipe Key   P/R
Storage Key   R
Schedule Key   1
Utensil Key   Spoon

Heavenly Mashed Potatoes

These get this name for several reasons. They can be prepared ahead of time, and even frozen. But it is truly their taste that makes them heavenly. Unfortunately, heavenly and low fat don't go together on this occasion. Your family will request these potatoes any time they know you are getting out the potato masher.

Amt	Item	Multiplied X	Total Quantity
9 lbs	Red Potatoes or Russets (peeled)		
½ lb	Butter or margarine		
16 oz	Cream Cheese		
4 ea	Green Onions		
2 + Cup	Whole Milk		
	Salt & Pepper		

Instructions:

Wash potatoes and cut into quarters. Cook in batches by putting approximately 2 inches of hot water in the bottom of the pan, adding potatoes to within two inches of top of pan, sprinkle with salt, cover with a tight fitting lid and steam until potatoes are folk tender. Monitor water level during cooking.

While potatoes are cooking, clean green onions and thinly slice…including the majority of the green top. Sauté in a small amount of butter over med low heat until the onions are limp.

Drain all water off of potatoes and let sit on burner to dry out the pan. You might need to mash the potatoes in batches to do a thorough job. Just put part of them in a bowl while you use a potato masher to start the process. Once you have all the lumps mashed out add a proportionate amount of butter and cream cheese. You can use an electric mixer to combine the ingredients from this point on. The heat from the potatoes will melt the cream cheese and butter. If you do need to set some of the potatoes aside, re-heat them briefly in the microwave before you start to mash them. After all the butter and cream cheese is worked into the potatoes, add the onions and the milk until the potatoes are the desired consistency. We prefer that they be more stiff, rather than runny, for ease in handling.

Salt and Pepper to taste. No gravy or additional butter is needed! Just reheat in a 325 degree oven for 30 to 40 minutes and serve. These can be placed in disposable ½ size hotel pans and go directly to the chafing dish to heat….or from oven to chafer.

Recipe Key	P/R
Storage Key	R/F
Schedule Key	1+ or 2
Utensil Key	Spoon

Green Chile Rice & Cheese Casserole
24 Servings

Another unique dish shared with us by a client that guests of all ages enjoy.

Amt	Item	Multiplied X	Total Quantity
4 C	Brown Rice uncooked		
3 LBS	Jack cheese – shredded		
4 C	Sour Cream		
28 oz	Canned Green Chilies		
1.5 C	Sharp Cheddar Cheese		
1 C	Medium Red Salsa		

Instructions

Cook the rice and drain if necessary. Combine with Sour Cream and salt to taste
Arrange half the mixture in the bottom of 3 ea 9 x 13 oblong pans
Clean the seeds from the canned chilies and place half in a layer over the rice, followed by a layer of the Jack Cheese.
Dot the cheese with spoonfuls of red salsa.
Layer the remaining chilies, then Jack cheese and remaining rice mixture.
Drop spoonfuls of red salsa over the rice mixture.
Dot with butter and sprinkle with grated Cheddar cheese
Bake at 350 for 30 to 40 minutes

Recipe Key	P/R
Storage Key	R/F
Schedule Key	1+ or 2
Utensil Key	Spoon

Drunken Green Beans
24 Servings

We know the French like wine with everything, and with this dish we understand why.

Amt	Item	Multiplied X	Total Quantity
2 Ea	1.5 lb Bags Frozen French Style Green Beans		
1 lb	Diced Bacon – Fried crisp		
2 Ea	Small cans Mushrooms (stem & pieces)		
1 ½ C	Red Wine		

Instructions:
Fry diced bacon until crisp, sauté with onions and mushrooms, add green beans and red wine, sauté until done.

Briefly reheat prior to serving.

Recipe Key	V
Storage Key	R
Schedule Key	1
Utensil Key	Spoon

Green Beans with Caramelized Red Onions

Amt	Item	Multiplied X	Total Quantity
1 ½ C	Olive oil		
6 ¼ Lbs	Red onions, thinly sliced		
4 ½ lbs	Slender green beans, trimmed (Can be frozen)		
6 ¼ Tbs	Balsamic vinegar		
3 ¼ Teas	Dried tarragon		

Instructions:
Heat 2/3 cup oil in heavy large skillet over medium-high heat. Add onions: sauté until deep brown, about 35 minutes. Season with salt and pepper. Cook beans in medium pot of boiling salted water until just crisp-tender, about 4 minutes. Drain; rinse under cold water until cool, then pat dry.

Whisk remaining ¾ cup oil in vinegar and tarragon in large bowl to blend. Add beans and onions and toss to coat. Season with salt and pepper. Serve warm or at room temperature.

Notes: The onions can be made ahead and then added with other ingredients prior to serving.

Recipe Key	V
Storage Key	R
Schedule Key	1
Utensil Key	Spoon

Green Beans with Sauteed Mushrooms
A simple but tasty side dish

24 Servings

Amt	Item	Multiplied X	Total Quantity
5 lbs	Frozen Green Beans		
1 C	Butter or Margarine		
4 ea	Garlic Cloves, minced		
2 lbs	Fresh Mushrooms		

Instructions:

Wash and clean mushrooms. Costco has big packages of portabellas that work well in this dish. If you use portabellas, discard the entire stem. Cut smaller sized mushrooms in slices. If using large ones, cut crosswise and rotate and cut crosswise again

Melt butter in a large skillet and add garlic cloves. If you will be cooking several batches, save enough garlic for the each batch. Add mushrooms and lightly sauté. Do not cook the mushrooms until they are limp, as they will cook while being reheated.

While the mushrooms are cooking add three inches of hot water to a large pot. When the water starts to boil add 2 ½ lbs of beans (if the pot will hold that many). When the water returns to a boil set the timer for 3 minutes. Check beans after that time…..they should be just slightly limp. Drain beans and put in bowl to cool. After all the beans and the mushroom mixture are cooked toss together and put in slide lock baggies. Refrigerate.

These can be heated on the stove top, in the chafer or a combination of both…depending on what quantity you are working with.

Recipe Key	V
Storage Key	R
Schedule Key	2-3
Utensil Key	Fork

Mixed Fruit

24 Servings

Our previous tried and true way of dealing with fruit, that will keep you from spending hours peeling and chopping is to visit Costco and purchase their 5 lb fruit tray. Our clients have used them repeatedly over the years and we have seen only one tray that was less than satisfactory in all that time. However, their price seems to have increased as the quantity decreased so this might be considered a toss up. In the summer we suggest adding a watermelon cut into chunks and additional grapes.... people seem to especially love fresh fruit when it is hot.

Amt	Item	Multiplied X	Total Quantity
5 lbs	Peeled and cut ready to eat fruit		
2 lbs	Red or green grapes		
1 ea	Seedless Watermelon		

If you decide to purchase whole fruit, use the following conversion to determine the amount of servable fruit you will have for each lb of purchase weight.
Melon may be cut into wedges and served separately, or the rind may be removed, the melon cut into chunks and combined with other fruits

Cantaloupe	1 lb at purchase will equal .52 lb ready to serve
Casaba	1 lb at purchase will equal .46 lb ready to serve
Honeydew	1 lb at purchase will equal .46 lb ready to serve
Persian	1 lb at purchase will equal .46 lb ready to serve
Watermelon	1 lb at purchase will equal .57 lb ready to serve
Strawberries	1 lb at purchase will equal .88 lb ready to serve
Apples	1 lb at purchase will equal .91 lb ready to serve
Bananas	1 lb at purchase will equal .65 lb ready to serve

Recipe Key	F
Storage Key	R
Schedule Key	1-2
Utensil Key	Tongs

Purchasing Quantitiy Guide for Miscellaneous Brunch Items

ITEM	QUANTITY TO SERVE 25	Multiplied X	Total Quantity
Sweet Rolls	2 ¼ dozen		
Coffee Cake	1 ea 12x18x2 pan		
Fruit Juice	6 oz glass 4 ¼ Qts 4oz glass 3 Qts		
Mini Bagels w/cream cheese	2 ¼ dozen		
Mini Muffins	2 ¼ dozen		
Melon – Cantaloupe	6 ea for ¼ melon serving		
Bananas	8 lbs		
Strawberries	7 lbs		
Mixed Fruit for fruit cup	4.5 lbs or 3 Qts. for 1/3 C serving		
Brown & Serve Sausage Links	3.5 – 4 lbs. 2 links per serving		
Sliced Baked Ham	9 – 10 lb with bone 7.5 lb boneless		

All Gone Champagne Punch

One of our clients shared this recipe with us. They served it in a fountain during the reception, and it was used in lieu of champagne for the toast. We didn't need to empty any glasses that night!

Amt	Item	Multiplied X	Total Quantity
1 C	Raspberry Brandy		
1 C	Brandy		
2 Qts	Ginger ale		
2 Bottles	Champagne		
2 to 3	Ice Molds		

Make ice molds by freezing water in plastic bowls.
Chill all ingredients prior to mixing.
Combine ingredients in the above ratio in the punch bowl. Remove ice mold from bowl by briefly immersing in a larger bowl, or sink, of hot water. Add one ice mold to punch bowl initially. Add an additional mold as needed as punch is replenished.

Angel Punch

This is the only non-alcoholic punch we recommend. It has a light citrus flavor and is very satisfying, but not too sweet.

Amt	Item	Multiplied X	Total Quantity
1 C	Sugar Syrup Mix 1 C sugar & ½ C water in pan, heat to dissolve sugar		
2 C	Lemon Juice (Real Lemon Bottled Lemon Juice works well)		
1 QT	Strong Green Tea (Use tea bags to make a strong tea)		
2 QT	White Grape Juice (Use frozen concentrate for ease)		
2 Qts	Chilled Club Soda		
2 to 3	Ice Molds (Make in plastic bowls)		

Make sugar syrup and tea ahead of time and refrigerate. Chill all ingredients and then mix in the above ratio just before serving.

Bar Guide

This is a bar set-up for 50 – I have included the complete list for reference only
Plan on adding if additional guests RSVP
If you don't plan on serving all types of liquor - add the quantity of the deleted liquor to one that you do plan on serving. Do the same for the mixers
If you know that you have a large beer drinking crowd, plan on doubling the quantities Same for wine

I would also have a extra back up bottle of the vodka, gin and tequila.
If you don't need, it you will have it for later

Beer	18	Cans	Cola	12	Cans
Light Beer	36	Cans	Diet Cola	12	Cans
Non-alcoholic Beer	3	Cans	7-Up	6	Cans
Tequila	1	Bottle large	Diet 7-Up	3	Cans
Gin	1	Bottle large	Club Soda	3	Liters
Rum	1/2	Bottle	Ginger ale	3	Liters
Scotch	1/2	Bottle	Tonic	6	Liters
Vermouth	1	Bottle	Bloody Mary Mix	2	Qts
Vodka	1/2	Bottle	Orange Juice	1	Gal
Whiskey	1/2	Bottle	Cranberry Juice	1	Qt
White Wine*	2	Bottles	Grapefruit Juice	1	Qt
Wine- Blush*	2	Bottles	Margarita Mix	3	Qts
Wine Red*	2	Bottles			

*Adjust according to number of people who will be drinking wine.

Figure 2 glasses per hour per person drinking wine.
750ml bottle of wine will provide 10-12 servings; A one liter bottle will serve 12 -14

The rule of thumb for the drinks is
Beer - 1 beer per hour per beer drinking guest - which I would at least double
Wine - 2 glasses of wine per hour per wine drinking guest
Soda - 2 sodas per hour per soda drinking guest
Water - 1 bottle per guest (the H20 drinkers will drink the non H20 drinkers water)

Champagne 5 one liter bottles, or 3 magnums
We normally only put in about 4 oz of bubbly, it looks fairly full, but doesn't waste too much.

THE POTLUCK – "How to get by with a little help from your friends"

Another solution for providing food is to have a Potluck reception.
You will use most of the tools already covered so far, and a potluck is quite manageable as long as you are organized and prepared. The upside is that your food costs will be reduced, the downside is that it could lend an air of uncertainty up to a certain point– depending on if your game plan is "tight" or "loose".
Don't forget to use the men. They love to be included and can do some of the heavy work

Where to start?

Designate two friends to be the organizational team for the Potluck. The mother of the bride and/or groom can certainly be involved but will need additional help as the time for the event draws closer.

They will be the contacts for communication with guests regarding the **WHW**

WHW = **W**ho is bringing **h**ow much of **w**hat type of dish.

Some points to ponder before moving forward:

1 How will you communicate to the guests that you would like them to bring food?

> The easiest way to request that guests bring food is to include a brief note with the invitation. One of the brides that we worked with chose to give guests an option of providing some sort of dish for the reception in lieu of a gift.

2 Who are you going to ask to participate?

> By using the invitation as a means of communicating, you can also control who receives the request or not; eg, the out-of-town guests, work acquaintances, etc.

3 Will you assign specific dishes to individuals or let them volunteer what they would like to bring?

Moving forward with the assumption that you will include a note in the invitation:

A) The information on the note should include:

The meal that will be served at the reception:

Brunch, Luncheon, Appetizers and Finger Foods, or Dinner

B) Email or phone number for Potluck Coordinators with a request that the guest contact one of the coordinators for more details, as soon as possible, if they would like to contribute a dish.

Do not request that they fill out and return the form – it is difficult enough to get guests to RSVP for the reception itself.

Once a guest contacts the team the relevant information can be exchanged. Tracking the WHW is covered later is this section.

C) We have found that is works best not to try to over manage what the guests will bring. They will either have a favorite dish they would like to contribute, or they plan on dropping by the local supper market to pick up a fruit or cheese platter. It is amazing how well balanced the food selections are when guests are able to choose their contribution. It is also amazing how fantastic many of the dishes taste!

The scenario that we recommend is to provide the meat course(s), if appropriate for the meal, and let guests decide what type of side dish they would like to bring. However, if you want to ask certain groups to bring specific food, you would make that request when they contact the Potluck Coordinator.

What Do You Do Next?

Coordinator's Tools

Determine what categories of foods you will be serving.

Appetizer
Vegetable Trays
Salad
Vegetable
Meat & Cheese Tray
Cheese and Fruit Tray
Rice or Potato
Bread

Fruit

Soft Drinks

Water (always serve water, no matter what time or type of party you have planned)

Ice

Assign a number to each type of dish that is going to be served and use the number in the column **D** when you fill in the volunteer's information.

For example - you are serving appetizers, salad, meat and cheese trays, bread, fruit and soft drinks.

> Appetizer = 1
>
> Salad = 2
>
> Meat and cheese tray = 3
>
> Bread = 4
>
> Fruit = 5
>
> Soft drinks = 6

This will provide an easy to use sort tool that will enable you to see exactly how much you have for each type of dish at any given time.

Each coordinator should maintain a contact list that includes the following information:

(We highly recommend using Excel if it is available; information from multiple sources can be combined and it provides sorting capabilities that save a lot of time.)

A Name	B Phone	C Email	D Category & Dish Description	E # of Servings	F Hot Or Cold	F 3 Week Follow up	G 2 Week follow up w / detail	H 1 Week Final Follow up

Fill in the columns as follows:

A-C Fill in the name and contact information as the responses come in.

D If guests know what they would like to bring the Dish Description column is completed.

If they don't have a preference, but ask what is needed, the coordinator could ask them if they would like to prepare one of the recipes we include in this book (don't forget the simple things like Relish trays, Meat and Cheese Trays, Cheese and Fruit trays, etc.).

> Note: the recipes are for 24 servings – the option of modifying the recipe should be offered if the higher quantity is overwhelming.

Or, the guest could be asked to bring any of the sundry items that might be needed. Ex: bread, butter, soft drinks, water, etc.

E Guests can volunteer to provide the number of servings their recipe makes; if they ask how much is needed we recommend using any multiple of 8 if that feels comfortable to them.

F Three weeks prior to the wedding an email or phone call reminder should be sent to each person bringing a dish. Include the information that additional details will be sent the following week.

> Between the 3rd and 2nd week before the event the coordinators should decide how many people will be needed to receive the food arriving at the site, which will be determined by how many guests are bringing food. Additional organizational ideas are included in the Chapter IX

The Most Important Factor at This Point – will the ceremony and reception take place at the same location or different locations? The difference between the two will affect the timing between when the food is dropped off and when the buffet service begins; the number of people doing preparation will need to be adjusted accordingly.

Possible Scenarios:
Picture this: The wedding is at the church and the reception is at the Masonic Lodge. 75 – 100 guests are attending and 25 people arrive at the Masonic Lodge kitchen within 8 minutes of each other; each carrying one of eight different types of dishes.

There is one person in the kitchen trying to talk to the first person through the door. The people carrying dishes behind her are eager to get back out to dining area because the bride and groom are due at any time. So they just set the dishes down and leave. Not all of the dishes will fit on the buffet at one time; consequently there will be different types of dishes scattered all over the kitchen. And once the serving starts, the food on the buffet will need to be replenished rapidly; there will be no time to go through that assortment of dishes spread out all over the kitchen counters to find the type of food needed. Help!!!!

> The kitchen should be organized with a person assigned to oversee each group of 2 to 3 types of dishes; arranging those groups on the buffet, organizing the backup in the kitchen and replacing empty dishes on the buffet as needed. Smooth……

Here is the 2nd scenario; it is a true story – Aunt Maude has committed to make her famous Caesar salad; the wedding guest list tops 300, Aunt Maude owns a restaurant - even does some catering (leading to very erroneous assumptions being made). She walks in with a bag of Caesar salad greens and one bottle of her famous salad dressing. Had there been no plan for food drop off, she would have put down her grocery bag and left. But, the person responsible for the salads knew when she saw one bag of lettuce (instead of 15) that the backup plan needed to go into action. Oh yes!! There is always a back up plan, but more about that later.

G. Phone or email the 2 week confirmation.
Include the following information:

> 1) Where the food should be delivered and the **name of the person** they should connect with in the kitchen. (Because our memories tend to be poor sometimes – a **master list of the food categories and the contact name will be posted by the door leading into the kitchen on the special day.**)

> 2) Recommend the appropriate sized **disposable** serving dish See chapter VIII

> 3) Include instructions to mark any **non disposable dishes** with **a name and phone number.**

> 4) Include suggested methods to keep food hot or cold; See the FAQ section
> (If hot food arrives hot it will shorten and simplify the preparation process)

5) **If the dish cannot be maintained at serving temperature, request that any reheating instructions be written on a small piece of paper and taped to the top the container.**

6) Also include the fact that any non-disposable containers **will not** be cleaned before it is picked up at the end of the function.

H...Phone or email final reminder 1 week prior to the event.

If emailing, include a request that guests send a return email confirming that they are bringing their dish to the function. If phoning, the purpose of the call is the confirmation.

Note: It is amazing how many people assume that the bride or groom's families just "know" that they will be there and therefore don't bother responding to RSVP requests. Fortunately, guests who commit to bringing food seem to be a little more willing to communicate; the responses should be fairly accurate. But, having a confirmed list of food providers is one of the biggest stress reducers possible!

Now we are going to back up a few weeks to and lay out the back up plan.

Three weeks before the wedding you should have a fairly accurate idea of how much food is being provided by the guests. Use the charts in Chapter VI to verify the quantities that will be needed for the function.

If there is not enough of one of the categories of food, determine how the gap will be filled.

There are numerous options, not necessarily listed in order or preference:

Ask a friend to provide the additional item or quantity needed.

Ask someone who has committed to making that dish if quantities could be increased.

Provide the dish yourself.

Order the food from a restaurant that offers multi-serving take out service (more and more mainstream restaurants are offering this service).

Substitute a similar item using prepared food picked up from Costco, Sam's Club, etc.

The one thing to keep in mind about the food in general is that not everyone is going to eat a portion of everything so you have leeway; if you a little more of this and a little less of that it will work just fine. The important issue is that you have enough food overall.

PLAN ON PROVIDING THE FOLLOWING ITEMS.

1) Multiple serving utensils for every food category. Review your list and multiply the number of categories by 3 or 4 (about how many dishes you will have on the buffet on one time).

2) Backup serving trays and bowls – because some of the food will arrive in baggies.

3) Kale, parsley or other decorative garnishes – they can be tucked around food for a very professional presentation.

4) Ice chests filled with ice if you don't have adequate refrigerator space for those items which should be kept cold until serving time. Especially salads with mayonnaise, fresh vegetables (request that they be brought in baggies so they fit in the ice chests or refrigerator; and allow time to arrange on the platters – or invite the person bringing them to return after the ceremony to arrange them.. ☺

5) Plastic grocery bags to carry the non-disposable serving dishes home.

6) Slide Lock Baggies – for any leftover food.

THE BACKUP PLAN

On the day of the function mishaps can occur....someone doesn't show up with their dish, or not as much as they committed to make. The ice is low and the reception still has a few hours to go. People are drinking water but not the punch.

Solution: when the backup box is being assembled it should include $50.00 in cash tucked in an envelope. Whatever the glitch – send someone to the store to purchase items needed; you will have enough unique dishes that no one will notice if you put out a dish or two straight from the grocery store deli.

ON THE DAY OF THE EVENT

Organization is the key to the function running smoothly.

Allow yourself or your designated person as much time as possible to put everything together.

Hopefully the previous communication with the guests providing food will ensure that at least some of the dishes arrive ready to be placed on the buffet. However, you must allow time to prepare or arrange those that are not. Also some items might need to be reheated.

> If the wedding ceremony and reception take place at the same location, people will be dropping off food prior to the ceremony. **Post a master list of the food categories and the contact name by the door leading into the kitchen on the special day.)**

> Draw up a map of the kitchen, which includes the holding area for each category of food and display it prominently where anyone walking into the kitchen will see it – if the contact person is not available the food can be placed in the appropriate area. Being organized at this point will lessen confusion later.

Having one or two people able to work during the wedding ceremony is strongly recommended. The hot entrees need to be heated during this time, the chafing dishes set up, etc. Because the friends and family of the bridal party want to see the ceremony, asking a friend of a friend is sometimes the best solution. Perhaps a good friend of one of the organizers who doesn't know the bride's or groom's family would be willing to help for a few hours.

You will have your kitchen map drawn, the buffet setup is laid out and you know exactly which dishes need to be preheated or arranged on platters etc, you have set up a task list and other organizational tools provided in Chap IX and XI. Everything Is Organized. It will be easy for someone who knows their way around a kitchen to step in and help out.

MISC
Desserts:
Sometimes desserts will appear in the kitchen - we have yet to figure that one out. Perhaps someone doesn't like wedding cake, or they want to show off their special recipe for a trifle.   When everyone has had the opportunity to visit the buffet for seconds, remove the serving dishes and then set aside one end of the buffet table to set out any additional desserts. Include small serving plates, napkins and utensils. Left- over fruit salad from the buffet can also be placed in this area.

"TO GO"

A new convenience is the large selection of menu items offered as catered "to go" items; large quantity servings from restaurants, supermarkets, delicatessens, pizza parlors, and specialty stores, etc. Organic, vegetarian and ethnic foods are also readily available

Your menu selection could consist of a mix of "To Go" entrees with homemade appetizers, side dishes and salads, or, vice-versa. The possibilities are unlimited. Another possibility is the complete meal could consist of "To Go" items.

There can also a cost advantage of ordering prepared items "To Go". A substantial portion of a caterer's budget is for the labor needed for the event. The cost the food and its preparation usually is budgeted at approximately 40% of the total cost. You are providing the labor that would account for the other 40-60%; consequently you can have exceptional dishes and still keep the cost down. In some instances it is also more economical to order "To Go" dishes because restaurants purchase food at wholesale prices. The added bonus for you- these items are then removed from your "to do" list and many restaurants will deliver if your order exceeds a certain dollar amount.

The following list is examples of various dishes, with actual prices, that can be ordered in large quantities that could work perfectly on your buffet. Check with any of your favorite local food establishments to see if you can order large serving quantities of food "to go", they already prepare most dishes in bulk and would just have to use a larger container for packaging. Just make sure you have enough oven space, or helpers, to heat the hot dishes as needed.

Also, be sure to include any "To Go" quantities when computing the quantity of food you need. You will be able to stretch the number of servings of each dish if you serve more than one type of dish in a particular category

To find restaurants that offer catered type dishes "To Go" you have the option of checking out a favorite local establishment, using the yellow pages and using the internet. For the latter, use a search engine such as Google. Type the phrase restaurant to go catering menu and your city in the search blank. The first page usually contains city search results that don't necessarily match what you want. Go back a few pages and you will find exactly what you are looking for. When the site opens look for a catering menu link and then look for menu items that can be purchased in large quantity servings or by the pound. If you see individual servings quoted the company doesn't provide the service you need.

If you have a favorite dish at a local restaurant that you would like to us it won't hurt to ask the manager if it could prepared in the quantity you need and packaged in a large "go' container…you will never know unless you ask.

Note: The following list consist of "To Go" items from menus from various restaurants in different parts of the country. Although they offer an excellent example of the food available, they might not reflect the cost of items in your area.

APPETIZERS

TOASTED RAVIOLI-50 pcs   Cheese filled with Tomato Sauce for Dipping 49.95

SHRIMP COCKTAIL-65 pieces   with cocktail sauce & honey glaze 129.95

ASSORTED CROSTINI PLATTER-40 pieces   tomato & feta cheese, caramelized onion & Asiago cheese, artichoke romano cheese 49.95

SCAMPI STYLE PRAWNS-65 pieces   **129.95**

STUFFED MUSHROOM CAPS-36 pcs   Filled with blended crab and shrimp, topped with a light cream sauce 49.95

COCKTAIL SIZE MEATBALLS-50 pieces   In or famous Original Sauce 39.95

ANTIPASTO TRAY, serves 10   Italian meats, chees, vegetables, olives and peppers 59.50

ITALIAN SAUSAGE (cocktail cut) - 50 pcs   Grilled with peppers and onions 44.95

HOT HORS D' OEUVRES -*With Cooking Instructions - Served from Your Oven*

SHRIMP $75
Grilled - 50 marinated shrimp with herb chili oil
Coconut - 50 seasoned shrimp with citrus and nut
Parmesan - 50 seasoned shrimp with herbs & citrus zest

PUFF PASTRIES $70   60 pastries filled with a variety of: Rosemary Chicken, Roasted Vegetables, Crab & Herb.

MUSHROOMS $75   60 mushrooms filled with a variety of: Spinach & Pecan, Crab, Italian Sausage

CRAB CAKES $75   50 cakes made with herbs.

BBQ MEATBALLS $60   75 meatballs with BBQ sauce

BRIE CHEESE $85   Our Signature Dish! Apples, pecans & cranraisins in pastry crust Served with crackers

BEEF BROCHETTE $80   50 skewers in a teriyaki marinade.

THAI CHICKEN SKEWERS $75   50 chicken skewers - marinated in a mild sweet Thai chili sauce

SALADS AND SUCH

HOUSE SALAD-serves 10   fresh greens tossed with olives, onions, tomatoes & cheese.on the side 18.95

CAESAR SALAD - Serves 10 Traditional recipe with Romao Cheese Croutons and Cascone's Caesar Dressing on the side   16.95

ITALIAN OLIVE SALAD, priced per pound   Green Italian olives, carrots, celery and garlic marinated in olive oil with herbs and spices 5.95

ROASTED VEGETABLE ASSORTMENT serves 10   24.95

TOMATO & MOZZARELLA SALAD for 10 36.00

PEAR SALAD VINAIGRETTE, serves 10
with Spinach and Walnuts and bleu cheese crumbles in red wine 29.95

COBB SALAD   Diced egg, tomatoes, blue cheese, bacon, chicken and avocado on a bed of greens with ranch & blue cheese dressing on the side. *Large: $70 (Serves 25 - 40)*

CHINESE CHICKEN SALAD Chicken, water chestnuts, pea pods, bell peppers, bean sprouts and rice noodles on a bed of greens with Oriental dressing. *Large: $70 (Serves 25 - 40)*

ISLAND CHICKEN SALAD Tossed with a curry lime dressing, green onions, mangos & papayas garnish on bed of field greens. *Large: $70 (Serves 25 - 40)*

SPINACH SALAD Fresh spinach, mandarin oranges, chèvre, grilled chicken and toasted almonds with Cabernet vinaigrette. *Large: $70 (Serves 25 - 40)*

TROPICAL FRUIT SALAD Pineapple, mangos, papayas, oranges, grapes, blueberries & currents on field greens with a citrus honey vinaigrette *Large: $70 (Serves 25 - 40)*

CAESAR SALAD, POTATO SALAD, PASTA, COLESLAW, GREEN SALAD
Large $60 *serves 25 – 40*

FIELD GREEN SALAD: candied pecans, cranaisins, and blue cheese with port dressing. **Large $65** *serves 25 – 40*

COLD PLATTERS
Large serves 25 – 40

FRESH VEGETABLES   Large $60

FRESH FRUITS   Large $60

IMPORTED AND DOMESTIC CHEESE & CRACKERS   Large $80

ASPARAGUS With rosemary, sun-dried tomatoes & goat cheese. Large $80

TORTA RUSTICA Layers of grilled vegetables, basil, spinach and cheese baked in pastry $65.00 Serves 25-30

POACHED SALMON   Fillet with capers, onions, lemons, tomatoes & dill sauce. $80.00

CHILLED SHRIMP PLATTER Beautifully decorated and served with tangy cocktail sauce **$140**

MINI CROISSANTS A dozen of any combination: Turkey, Ham, Roast Beef, Tuna Salad & Chicken Salad. $25.00

MINI WRAPS A dozen of any combination: Turkey w/ Artichoke, Ham w/ Swiss, Chicken Salad, Grilled Vegetable $25.00

GINI GINGER CHICKEN   A dozen delicious blend chicken & ginger raisin bread. $25.00

ENTREES AND PASTA
Party Size $31.00 Serves 12-14 (applies to all the following entrees that don't have an individual price)

BEEF STEW Made with specially cut sirloin beef and slowly simmered to perfection with celery, onions, carrots and potatoes.

CREAMY CHICKEN ENCHILADAS A just-right combination of chicken, onion, green chilies and cheeses wrapped in flour tortillas and smothered with a creamy sauce.

CHICKEN & GREEN BEAN Long grain and wild rice are perfectly matched with chicken and green beans and simmered with onion, pimiento, mushrooms and water chestnuts. It's then baked with creamy celery and sour cream sauce, cheese and seasonings.

CHICKEN & WILD RICE Chicken and mushrooms are gently sautéed and baked with wild rice, broth of chicken, Italian dressing, and sour cream for a perfect entrée.

CHICKEN TETRAZZINI Chicken and noodles are cooked and teamed with pimiento, our creamy mushroom sauce, and topped with parmesan cheese.

CHICKEN POT PIE Chicken and broth are mixed with onions, peas and carrots. All this is added to our creamy sauce, seasoned and placed in pastry shell and topped with pastry. Just bake and enjoy.

SIGMON CHICKEN PIE A hearty recipe of chicken, chicken broth and seasonings slow cooked, then piled into a pie and topped with pie crust and baked. When serving, top with a light chicken gravy if you desire.

HAM, BACON, SAUSAGE OR TOMATO MUSHROOM QUICHE Delicious for breakfast, lunch or dinner. 16.00.

CLASSIC LASAGNA Meaty, red and cheesy are words for this one! Lasagna noodles are alternately layered with sauce made with ground beef and bell peppers, onions, tomatoes, parmesan, mozzarella and Romano cheeses. *Also available are Vegetable Lasagna and Chicken Lasagna*

MUSHROOM-PEPPER STEAK Mm Good is the only description for this one! Beef, peppers, onions, celery are sautéed, then covered with a tasty sauce. Serve over rice.

CHICKEN DIVAN By popular request we crated this dish and it is delicious! Chicken and broccoli are layered with a sour cream sauce and topped with parmesan cheese.

SAUSAGE JAMBALAYA Smoked sausage, rice, tomatoes and spices make this a delightful dinner change. We also have this available for you to make yourself.

MACARONI 'N CHEESE This one is better than average! Elbow macaroni is baked in our own sharp Cheddar cheese sauce and topped with more cheese.

RED CHICKEN STEW Southern tradition abounds in our tasty ketchup based stew. Tender chicken chunks teamed with sweet onion and boiled egg. Serve over rice if desired.

BACKBONE AND RICE Pork Boston Butt and onions, simmered 'till tender and combined with rice and seasonings.

ITALIAN CHICKEN ROLL-UPS, People in a hurry will love these tender chicken breast, ham and cheese roll-ups to pull out of the freezer and cook. Slice into pretty medallions when company comes. Three roll-ups 10.99

SHRIMP & GRITS A generous amount of shrimp simmered in garlic cheese grits and other seasonings.

CHICKEN ALFREDO A wonderful blend of Parmesan, Romano and Cheddar cheeses combined with tender chicken, broccoli, herbs in a sauce with Fettuccini noodles.

CHICKEN SPEDINI - 12-3 piece skewers Marinated chicken breast lightly breaded, skewered and grilled, topped with our Amogio Marinade 59.95

CHICKEN LIMONATA ELAINA - 12 pieces Whole Boneless Breast of Chicken in a light creamy white wine, lemon, butter sauce 65.00

WHOLE BEEF TENDERLOIN, serves 15 with peppercorn sauce and tomato amogio 225.00

SHRIMP SPEDINI-24 pieces Large prawns marinated, lightly breaded & grilled, basted with our special lemon garlic marinade 85.00

VENETIAN EGGPLANT - 24 pieces eggplant rolls stuffed with angel hair pasta and ricotta cheese in creamy tomato sauce 39.95

ITALIAN SAUSAGE CASSEROLE - 24 pieces Grilled with peppers, onions and potatoes 49.95

CHICKEN PARMIGIANA - 12 piece Boneless chicken breast lightly breaded in Modiga style crumbs, sauteed then topped with Mozzarella and pasta sauce 49.95

SAUTEED EGGPLANT - 12 pieces breaded, seasoned with crumbs and romano cheese, served with sliced tomatoes and tomato sauce on the side 39.95

The following are full dinner prices for 10

BBQ TRI TIPS Baked beans, buttered corn, green salad & rolls. 139.50

ROAST PORK LOIN Plum sauce, vegetables, potatoes, salad & rolls 139.50

STUFFED CHICKEN BREAST   Spinach, sun-dried tomatoes and cheese sliced and topped with a champagne basil sauce, Lemon Thyme Rice, Green Beans, Field Green Salad and Rolls 165.50

CHICKEN - CITRUS, PICATTA or MARSALA   Rice, vegetables, green salad & rolls 139.50

SEARED SALMON With basil Dijon marinade, Garlic mashed potatoes, julienne vegetables, field green salad, rolls & butter 149.50

Pastas by the Pan

PASTA WITH TOMATO SAUCE - Serves 8-10   Your choice of Spaghetti, Shells, Mosticiolli or Fettuccini pasta 39.95

PASTA WITH MEAT SAUCE - Serves 8 – 10 Your choice of Spaghetti, Shells, Mosticiolli or Fettuccini pasta with our Meat Sauce 45.95

PASTA WITH ALFREDO SAUCE - Serves 8 – 10 Your choice Spaghetti, Shells, Mosticiolli or Fettuccini pasta with our Alfredo Sauce 49.95

PASTA WITH MARINARA SAUCE - Serves 8 – 10   Your choice of Spaghetti, Shells, Mosticiolli or Fettuccini pasta with Marinara Sauce 49.95

BAKED MOSTICIOLLI CASSEROLE - Serves 10 – 12 Penne pasta tossed with sliced sweet Italian sausage, ricotta, mozzarella topped with parmesan cheese and our Original pasta sauce, then baked 49.95

BAKED SPAGHETTI (PASTA AL FORNO) - serves10 baked with salami, eggplant, seasoned ground beef, peas, mozzarella, ricotta and parmesan cheese 55.95

CASCONE'S FAMOUS BAKED LASAGNA - Serves 8-10 Layers of pasta, meat and three cheeses. Baked with our original pasta sauce 49.95

BAKED CANNELONI - Serves 8-10 Filled with a mixture of blended Ricotta cheese &Italian sausage, baked with Mozzarella and our house tomato sauce, 32 pieces 59.95

SHELLS MARINARA WITH BAY SHRIMP - Serves 10 ....59.95

CHEESE FILLED RAVIOLI - 60 pieces Served with tomato sauce 49.95

CHEESE FILLED RAVIOLI WITH MEAT sauce - 60 pieces 59.95

PENNE PRIMAVERA - serves 10 pasta tossed with fresh vegetables in a creamy tomato sauce 49.95

VEGETABLE CASSEROLES

Party Size $28.00 Serves 24 (applies to all the following vegetable dishes that don't have an individual price)

ASPARAGUS SOUFFLÉ A classic favorite that goes with any entrée. Asparagus, milk, egg and cheese.

SQUASH Market fresh squash and onions are sautéed and mixed with our creamy sauce and topped with bread crumbs and Cheddar cheese.

SQUASH AND ZUCCHINI BAKE Squash, zucchini, onions, pimiento baked with cheese and bread crumbs topping.

BROCCOLI A favorite, chopped broccoli is combined with a sauce made with mushrooms, carrots and milk, then topped with bread crumbs and Cheddar cheese.

CORN PUDDING Prepared the old fashion way, this pudding is perfectly seasoned to bring out the sweetness of the corn and to complement any entrée.

SWEET POTATO CRUNCH Any time of year you can count on our Sweet Potato Crunch to get rave revues. Pecans add the crunch.

WADMALAW ISLAND EGGPLANT PIE A simple, but great dish with a mixture of eggplant, egg, onion, bell pepper, Cheddar cheese, Worcestershire sauce.

SCALLOPED POTATOES Sliced potatoes layered with our creamy Cheddar cheese sauce.

GREEN BEAN CASSEROLE A classic. Fresh string beans layered with cream of mushroom soup and topped with fried onion rings make this a delight for any occasion.

CORNBREAD DRESSING A year 'round moist and delicious dish to serve with chicken, turkey or pork.

TOMATO PIE Fresh tomatoes, peppers and onions, layered in a pie crust with seasonings, and topped with sharp Cheddar cheese and salad dressing.

MEXICAN FOOD

Full Trays – server 30 to 40
29.95 - Rice, Beans, Salad –
29.95 - Shredded Beef or Chicken
89.95 - Chile Verde, Steak Ranchero, Pollo en Mole, Chili Colorado, Birria, Steak or Chicken Fajitas, Carnitas, Pollo a la Diabla, Puntas de Filete ala Mexicana
189.95 Shrimp Camarones a la Diabla o Rancheros

Side Order
Guacamole 5 lbs 29.50
Sour Cream 5 lbs 12.50
Salsa or Pico de Gallo 5 lbs 12.50
Corn Tortillas 1 dozen 3.50
Flour Tortillas 1 dozen 2.75
Chips Large Bag 20.00

We generally recommend about 1/4 - 1/3 pound per person for below salads.
Minimum order of 5 pounds.
Price per pound.

Legume/Grain Salads

Three bean salad with smoky molasses dressing 8.00
Spicy corn, black bean & peppers with chipotle vinaigrette 9.50; Add shrimp 10.00
Roasted beet & French green lentils with feta, walnuts, & house-preserved lemon vinaigrette 9.50
Quinoa with mango, almonds & curry vinaigrette 9.50
Very wild rice with dried fruit & cashews 9.50

Pasta/Noodle Salads

Fusilli with assorted vegetables & blue cheese dressing 9.00
Sesame noodle salad with asparagus 9.50; Add chicken 10.00
Farfalle salad Nicoise with olives, capers & sun-dried tomatoes 9.00; Add chicken 9.50
Pasta with corn, green beans, cherry tomatoes & pesto 9.50

Other Salads
Ask about other seasonal choices.
Classic potato salad with herbs 9.00
Fresh fruit salad 9.00
Celery root & Granny Smith apples with mustard vinaigrette 9.50
Chez Panisse Chicken Provencal with peppers, capers & olives 9.50
Caprese Salad of mixed heirloom tomatoes, fresh mozzarella & basil 9.50
Greek salad with tomatoes, cucumbers, feta, olives & oregano 9.50

BREAKFAST
Serves 10

CONTINENTAL $60. Pastries, fresh fruit and juice.

QUICHE $55   Sun-Dried Tomato, Basil & Goat Cheese, Grilled Vegetable & Gouda Cheese, Apple & Canadian Bacon, Spinach & Mushroom

BREAKFAST BURRITIOS $69.50 Scrambled Eggs, Chorizo & Cheese wrapped in Flour tortilla and served with fresh fruit and juice, side Tabasco

SIDES $25.00 BACON or SAUSAGE
BREAKFAST POTATOES

PLANNING

RECIPE SELECTION WORKSHEET

RECIPE QUANTITY WORKSHEET

You will be using the worksheets and following these steps to ensure that you have an adequate, but not excessive, amount of food for your function.

1) Determine how many menu items to serve
2) Choose recipes
3) Compute the appropriate modifications regarding the number of recipes to prepare, based on the guest count.
4) Determine the recipe adjustments based on the number of recipes selected in each classification
5) Calculate number of times to modify each base recipe
6) Multiply recipe ingredients
7) Compile Shopping List

APPETIZERS

If you are serving appetizers prior to, or in place of a buffet, use the following rule of thumb to determine the quantity of appetizer *pieces* you will need *per person*, based on the length of time you will be serving.

½ Hour		1 Hour		2-3 Hours	
Hot	Cold	Hot	Cold	Hot	Cold
5	3	6	5	8	7

Choose the worksheet closest to your guest count

Enter your selections from the master recipe file

MENU for 25	Recipe
Appetizer	
Entrée	
Rice/Pasta	
Salad	
Vegetable	

Select 2 of the following 4 options

1 Fruit	
2 Cheese Platter	
3 Vegetable Tray	
4 Relish Tray	

MENU for 50	Recipe
Appetizer	
Appetizer	
Entrée	
Entrée	
Rice/Pasta	
Salad	
Vegetable	
Select 2 of the following 4 options	
1 Fruit	
2 Cheese Platter	
3 Vegetable Tray	
4 Relish Tray	

MENU for 75	Recipe
Appetizer	
Appetizer	
Appetizer	
Entrée	
Entrée	
Rice/Pasta	
Salad	
Salad	
Vegetable	
Select 3 of the following 4 options	
1 Fruit	
2 Cheese Platter	
3 Vegetable Tray	
4 Relish Tray	

MENU for 100	Recipe
Appetizer	
Appetizer	
Appetizer	
Entrée	
Entrée	
Rice/Pasta	
Salad	
Salad	
Vegetable	
Fruit	
Cheese Platter	
Vegetable Tray	
Relish Tray	

MENU for 125	Recipe
Appetizer	
Appetizer	
Appetizer	
Appetizer	
Entrée	
Entrée	
Rice/Pasta	
Salad	
Salad	
Salad	
Vegetable	
Fruit	
Cheese Platter	
Vegetable Tray	
Relish Tray	

MENU for 150+	Recipe
Appetizer	
Appetizer	
Appetizer	
Appetizer	
Entrée	
Entrée	
Rice/Pasta	
Rice/Pasta	
Salad	
Salad	
Salad	
Vegetable	

Vegetable

Fruit

Cheese Platter

Vegetable Tray

Relish Tray

The blank table for your use if you are compiling your own combinations

Menu Item	Recipe

WORKSHEET TO DETERMINE RECIPE QUANTITIES

You have a rough guest count and have selected your recipes.
If you have selected two meat entrees and are having 150 guests, you don't want to purchase enough of each meat for 150 servings. Because then you will have enough meat to serve 300!

And it is going to take your helpers quite a while to bag up all that left over food.

So we are going to help you determine how much of each recipe will be needed to adequately serve the number of guests you are expecting.

By now you should have completed your Recipe Selection worksheet. Using it, and this table, you will Compute the quantity of each recipe you will need to prepare. There is one additional step involving your original recipe which you will be instructed to complete.
The directions for this task are located on the last page of this section.

Essentially, you will select the quantity to serve for your total guest count and then divide by the total number of dishes in that particular category

The tables we use are all related. If you plan on adding more items than indicated, just remember to decrease the quantities of the other foods you are preparing. When a variety of foods are available, people tend to serve themselves less than if they were sitting down to a single course meal.
The exception to this is young men ages 13 to 22.

There are two ways to compute how much food to prepare.

Food that is computed by volume will use a simple equation.

Example

Number of Guests 150	Quantity to serve 150	Divided by total number of dishes selected for a particular category	Total quantity of each menu item to serve
Entrée – Ham w/Cola Sauce	50 lb	2	= 25 lbs
Entrée –Smoked Turkey	50 lbs	2	= 25 lbs
Salad – Green	10 lbs greens	3	= 3.33 lbs
Salad - Potato (purchased)	6 gals	3	= 2 gals
Salad – 3 Bean	4 gals	3	= 1.3 gals

Food prepared using recipes will be similar, but the adjustment will be made in the portion selection column.

Number of Guests 150	N/A	Divided by total number of dishes in a particular category	Multiply recipe portion to serve	Divide by 25 (our recipe servings) **Transfer this figure to the Multiplied X column in the recipe**
Entrée – Lasagna		2	75	3
Entrée – Mojito Chicken		2	75	3
Potato Salad		3	50	2
Pasta Salad		3	50	2
Broccoli Salad		3	50	2

Feel free to adjust these figures if you are serving a dish that you feel will be more popular than another.

For instance, you might want to increase the Pasta Salad recipe, but would then decrease one of the others.

If you have a group of very heavy eaters you might want to slightly increase the quantities. My son was a football player in high school and college; his single friends made quite a dent in the buffet at his wedding reception.

Worksheet to compute food quantity by volume

Number of Guests Item quantity determined by volume	Quantity to serve total number of guests	Divided by total number of dishes selected for a particular category	Total quantity of each menu item to serve

Worksheet to compute number of recipes by category

Number of Guests Recipe		Divided by total number of dishes selected for a particular Category	Multiply recipe portion to serve	Divided by recipe portion of 25 **Transfer this figure to the Multiplied X column in the recipe**

Final Step

Have printed copies of your selected recipes available.

1) Using the menu selections and completed computations for the adjustments, transfer the number from the last worksheet column to the **Multiplied X Column** on your recipe page for each recipe.

2) Multiply each ingredient by the figure in the **Multiplied X** column and write the adjusted amount in the **Total Quantity** column of your recipe. Now you are ready to build your shopping list.

GETTING ORGANIZED

SHOPPING LIST

PURCHASING TIPS

THE PREPERATION SCHEDULE

COOKING LARGE QUANITITES OF FOOD

MEAT WEIGHTS

THE SHOPPING LIST

Going shopping with an organized list will save you energy and help minimize your frustration level.

We have set up a master form with a section for each food category in the grocery store. As you compile your grocery list, enter each item under the appropriate header and your list will be organized when you are ready to shop.
By this point you should have selected and adjusted your recipe quantities. Write the item and quantity in the appropriate area of the form.

Also, place the abbreviation for the recipe in the space provided by each item.

Notice there is a column with an **H** next to the item on the form. Check your spices and sundry items; if you have an item in your cupboard; check this box so you don't purchase additional quantities.

Or, set up an Excel spreadsheet. Include columns for Item, Qty, Category, Recipe Abbreviation and H.

When you have entered the information for all the recipes, sort by Category; you will have an organized shopping list.

When shopping, you will be organized, which will save time and energy.

If you have chosen to prepare some recipes that can be frozen, simply cross those items off the list at the time of purchase.

You will also have a cross reference back to the recipe. If you are delegating cooking re-sponsibilities; sort the items by recipe while unpacking. Consult your shopping list and know exactly which recipe each item belongs to.

SHOPPING LIST

BREAD	H	QTY	RECIPE
DAIRY			

FRUIT	H	QTY	RECIPE
MEAT			

SUNDRY ITEMS	H	QTY	RECIPE

VEGETABLES	H	QTY	RECIPE

BEVERAGES	H	QTY	RECIPE
PAPER PRODUCTS			
ICE			

Purchasing Tips

Miscellaneous Items

Definitely check on-line resources for expanded variety and cost savings.

Visit your local "Dollar" store — many are starting to carry a variety of wedding items. Also check their website to for bulk ordering; ex: small vases to hold flowers arrangements for each table

Meats
Watch for sales. Most of the meats in our recipes will freeze for six months without a problem. To protect against freezer burn, place in freezer bags and remove as much air as possible.

Fruit
Buy seasonal fruits for the best cost savings. ie: don't plan on watermelon in December.
However, many fruits imported from South America are available year round.
Avoid frozen or canned fruits. They will have a serious impact on your budget and are not as appealing to your guests.

Vegetables
If you are having a function in mid to late summer, take advantage of your local farmer's market if possible. We suggest sending a helper shopping shortly before the closing time. The vendors will usually be willing to barter, and you will be able to get a better price for fresh goods. You will be buying larger quantities than the average consumer, in addition to saving the vendor the labor of returning the goods to their facility. So, it is a win-win situation.

Use frozen vegetables and add a sauce or garnish….economical way to "fill" up your guests.

Beverages
Watch for sales if you plan on serving canned sodas. They can be stored indefinitely if you have the space.
Sale prices usually are a better buy than case prices at the Big Box stores.

Consider purchasing a keg if you anticipate a large number of beer drinkers. The keg will be easier to handle than cases and cases of beer cans. It is also requires less space to ice down.

Miscellaneous Items
Buy the best quality you can afford. Some brand name products are just better than store brands.

THE PREP SCHEDULE

How to use the worksheet:

Use the Schedule key indicated at the bottom of each recipe and note the recipe name in the appropriately colored column.

As you line up your helpers, indicate their name in the appropriate space for that recipe.

You can also write yourself reminders for any tasks that you need to assign for the two days prior to the event in the last two columns.

SCHEDULE KEY

1+	1 month or more prior to function
5	5 days prior to function
4	4 days prior to function
3	3 days prior to function
2	2 days prior to function
1	1 day prior to function - friends only – not the bride or bride's mother

EXAMPLE for PREP SCHEDULE

1+ Prep Ahead & Freeze	5 Days Prior to Function	4 Days Prior to Function	3 Days Prior to Function	2 Days Prior to Function	1 Day Prior to Function	The Big Day
Recipe Name Sweet & Sour Sausage Balls Cook Mom	Recipe Name Sun-dried Tomato Spread Cook Nancy	Recipe Name Ham Glaze Cook Charlotte	Recipe Name Turkey Caesar Wraps Cook Peg	Recipe Name Roasted Potatoes w/Peppers Cook Peg		
Recipe Name Rosemary Chicken Cook Sharon	Recipe Name Cook	Recipe Name Cook	Recipe Name Cook		Recipe Name Ham – Cut off bone and place in baggies Cook Charlotte	

PREPERATION SCHEDULE

Prep Ahead & Freeze	Monday	Tuesday	Wednesday	Thursday	Friday	Saturday

PREPERATION SCHEDULE

Prep Ahead & Freeze	Monday	Tuesday	Wednesday	Thursday	Friday	Saturday

GUIDELINES FOR COOKING LARGE AMOUNTS OF FOOD

After you have selected the recipes that appeal to you, please read each one thoroughly.

Before you begin to cook, read the recipe from start to end, AGAIN.

Assemble all your ingredients for the recipe and pre-measure all spices, dry, and liquid items prior to assembling or cooking the dish.

You will be dealing with larger amounts of food than normal, and probably don't have the large pans, or the stove top and ovens, to accommodate these quantities. So, be aware that you will need to do some of the prep work in batches; to fit the pots and pans that you are using. We have found that food will brown or sauté faster if you don't overload or crowd the pan. So work with the food in manageable sized batches. The outcome will be better and you won't get frustrated wondering when the food in your overcrowded pan is going to start to resemble what the recipe calls for.

Cut pieces of food to be cooked together in similar sized pieces to ensure even cooking.

Have everything prepped and ready to go before you start to actually cook a specific recipe. This will ensure that you don't get to a point where something needs to be added, but due to the quantity involved, you are still chopping.

Use a food processor to do as much of the prep work as possible. If you are using recipes with items that are chopped or minced, and you don't own one, try to borrow one from a friend.

After cooling items, place in slide lock baggies to store in the refrigerator or freezer. The bags will lay flat and take up much less space.

Use extra large slide lock bags to marinate meats or vegetables. Just flip the bag over half way thru the process and all of the food will be evenly marinated. It will also reduce the amount of marinate required to cover the food.

Clear all decorative items and clutter off your counter tops prior to starting to cook. You will need room to place the cooked items to cool.

PURCHASE WEIGHTS OF MEAT

Use this table to determine the purchase weight of meat for the number of guests you are serving if you are not using a FFF recipe.

	Purchase Qty to serve 25	Purchase Qty to serve 50	Multiples of 50	Multiples of 25	Total Purchase Weight
BEEF					
Ground Beef 73% Lean	7.5	15			
Ground Beef 80% Lean	6.5	13			
Ground Beef 85% Lean	6	12			
Chuck Roast Boneless	9	18			
Chuck Roast w/Bone	11	22			
Rib Eye Roast	7.5	15			
Cubed Stew Meat	7.5	15 lbs			
Bottom Round Roast	9	18			
Boneless Rump Roast	9	18			
Boneless Sirloin Roast	9	18			
Short ribs	20	40			
Sirloin Steak Boneless	8	16			
Tenderloin	7	14			
T-Bone 8oz AP Portion	12.5	25			
12oz AP Portion	19	38			
PORK – FRESH					
Chops	12.5	17			
Ham Whole Boneless	10	20			
Ham Whole w/Bone	11	22			
Shoulder, Boston Butt Boneless	10	20			
Shoulder Boston Butt w/ Bone	10.5	21			
Shoulder Picnic Boneless	11	22			
Shldr. Picnic w/Bone	12.5	25			
Loin Roast Boneless	10	20			
Loin Roast w/Bone	12	24			
Sausage Bulk	7.5	15			
Sausage Links	4	8			
Spareribs	20	40			

POULTRY	Purchase Qty to serve 25	Purchase Qty to serve 50	Multiples of 50	Multiples of 25	Total Purchase Weight
PORK - CURED					
Bacon	3	6			
Canadian Bacon	5	10			
Ham - Boneless	7.5	15			
Ham w/Bone	10	20			
Ham, Fully Cooked, ready to eat	7.5	15			
Ham - Canned	7.5	15			
Shoulder, Boston Butt	8	16			
Shoulder, Picnic Boneless	9	18			
CHICKEN					
Fryer Parts					
½ Breast w/o back	8	16			
1 Drumstick & Thigh	10	20			
1 Drumstick	5	10			
1 Thigh	5.5	11			
2 Wings	7.5	15			
Chicken Whole					
Serving Portion ¼ Fryer	7 ea	14 ea			
Serving Portion ½ Fryer	12 ea	25 ea			
Whole, for Stewing	14	28			
Cooked – Diced	3 lbs 2 oz	6 lbs 4 oz			
TURKEY					
Whole for roasting	25 lbs	50 lbs			
Boneless Roll, Raw	9 lbs	18 lbs			
Boneless Roll, Cooked	7.5 lbs	15 lbs			
Breasts, whole , Raw	9.5 lbs	19 lbs			
Leg Quarters	9.5 lbs	19 lbs			
Turkey Ham Cooked	2.5 lbs	5 lbs			

Meat servings are 3 to 4 ounces AP per person unless otherwise noted.

SERVING PIECES FOR THE BUFFET

&

STOCKING THE KITCHEN

**Worksheets and Lists to ensure that everything is
on hand for the day of your event**

THE MASTER EQUIPMENT LIST

Serving Pieces

These are general suggestions for serving pieces. We recommend that you don't try to use your regular sized bowls and platters from home. Doing so will seriously impair the flow of the buffet and increase the time needed to serve all the guests. A list of recommended serving piece dimensions is included in this section.

Hors d'oeuvres, appetizers, wraps, and cheeses can be placed on large platters.

Footed glass cake stands stacked with wraps or appetizers will add dimension to the buffet.

Salads and cold vegetables should be placed in large bowls

Green salads are attractive in large pebble plastic opaque bowls

Fruits should be placed in wide shallow bowls

Breads and rolls work well in large baskets lined with napkins.

Vegetables are appealing laid on flat greens in large flat baskets.

Dips in medium glass bowls can be set in a large basket and chips added to surround the dip.

We suggest renting the chafers. For easy clean up use disposable foil pans. Two pans 10x12, approximately the size of a sheet of paper, will fit perfectly in the regular chafing pan. They can go right from the oven to the chafer and can be easily changed. And they go right from the buffet table to the garbage can. Price large bowls and platters at Smart & Final and **Cateringsupplies.com**; they have some items that can be used more than once and are reasonably priced.

Check out Michaels or your local craft super store for baskets…..many times you can purchase a basket for what it would cost to rent a platter.

You will also need serving implements for each dish. Plan on having two large forks or spoons for each dish you are serving. You can find nice serving sized implements at your local grocery or discount store for less than five dollars each. Although they are a plain design, they are very functional and can be used at home after the function.   Also plan on purchasing several small ice tongs, they are ideal for picking up pieces of cheese or relish tray items. If you are serving a green salad we highly recommend using the one piece combo salad servers……they allows guests to serve themselves salad without putting down their plates to pick up separate serving pieces. And again, plan on one for each side of the buffet.

The worksheet to help you determine exactly how many serving pieces you will need is also included in this section.

The Back-Up Box

This is the list of items you want on hand for preparation and clean-up if you are renting a facility for your function

☐ Plastic wrap

☐ Slide lock baggies

☐ Scissors

☐ Heavy duty clear tape

☐ Good sharp knives

☐ Matches or flicker style long lighter

☐ A pitcher

☐ 4 large spoons

☐ 2 extension cords

☐ Every dish towel and bath mat you own

☐ Sponges

☐ Pam Cooking Spray

☐ Foil

☐ Bottle of hand sanitizer

☐ 2 of your largest measuring cups

☐ Cutting boards

☐ First aid kit

☐ Paper doilies

☐ A heavy duty can opener

☐ 2 forks

☐ One or two small portable fans

☐ At least 2 hot pad holders

☐ SOS pads

☐ Aprons if you have them, visit Goodwill if you don't.

☐ Throw in a few plastic grocery bags from your last shopping trip.

☐ 2 rolls of paper towels (these might not fit in the box – put in a bag next to the box)

☐ 1 box of 35 gallon heavy duty garbage bags – the new flex ones are great

☐ 2 cork screws (we suggest the simple restaurant type – the others tend to break)

☐ Liquid dishwashing detergent (Use the dishwasher detergent to soak any pans with heavy baked on food; it uses an enzymatic action to dissolve the food and is slick)

☐ Disposable gloves – purchase a small box- the helpers can put them on to handle fruit, vegetables, and relishes. They will save a significant amount of time during both preparation and cleaning up.

SERVING PLATTERS, BOWLS, BASKETS AND UTENCILS

Before completing this table you need to determine how large a buffet you need to set up.

How many guests are you serving? How many food layouts (the complete menu selection) will you need to serve your guests in a reasonable time frame?

A rule of thumb

25 – 50 guests - 1 layout of food with serving from the front = 1 line

50 - 150 guests - 1 layout of food with guests moving on front and back sides = 2 lines

151 + guests - 2 layouts of food with guests moving on front and back sides = 4 lines

If you are setting up a double buffet with 2 identical layouts, the guests will start at the opposite ends of the table, on the front and back sides, and move toward the middle. Or, set up two separate buffets and have the DJ instruct the guests to proceed to the buffet nearest them.

Will one large dish be positioned to serve both sides of the table? If so, plan for 2 serving utensils for each serving piece. Or, if dishes will be mirrored front and back they will each need a serving piece.

For 50-150 guests, add 1 *additional serving piece for back-up preparation* for those menu items not served in a chafing dish. Add 2 extra pieces for back up for guest counts over 150.

Number of serving lines x number of serving pieces   Example: Potato Salad: 2 lines with 1 bowl for each line

Recipe	Serving Piece	Size	Number of Serving Lines	Number of Serving Dishes Per line	# of Back Up Pieces	= Total Qty	Purchase	Rent	Serving Utensil	Qty	Purchase	Rent
Potato Salad	Plastic Bowl	12 Qt	1	2		2	X		Spoon	4	x	
Rolls	Basket	18"	2	2		4	X		Tongs	4	X	
Green Salad	Salad Bowl	20 QT	1	1		1	X		Salad Servers	2	X	

Recipe	Serving Piece	Size	# of Lines	Number of Serving Dishes Per line	# of Back Up Pieces	= Total Qty	Purchase	Rent	Serving Utensil	Qty	Purchase	Rent

FRUGALLY FABULOUS Wedding Receptions

Recipe	Serving Piece	Size	# of Lines	Number of Serving Dishes Per line	# of Back Up Pieces	= Total Qty	Purchase	Rent	Serving Utensil	Qty	Purchase	Rent

SERVING PIECES
Suggested Sizes and Shapes to Accommodate Large Quantities of Food

TRAYS
Oval   16" X 12"
                  22" X 16"

Oblong   17" X 14"
                  24" X 18"

BASKETS
Round   16" – 24" Diameter   3"- 10" deep
Oblong   18" X 12" X 3"
                  18" X 30" X 3–1/2"
PLATTERS
Oval   14" X 10"
                  15" X 12"
                  17" X 13"
                  21" X 15"

Rectangular   10" X 14"
                  13" X 17"

Oblong   18", 20", 22", or 24"

BOWLS
Round   6"   18.8 oz
                  8"   1.65 Qts.
                  10"   5 lbs or 3.2 Qts
                  12"   5.8 Qts.
                  13"   10 lbs
                  15"   11.2 Qts
                  18"   20.2 Qts.
                  23"   40 Qts
Clamshell   12 oz
                  22 oz
                  5 Qt

UTENCILS
Serving Spoons   8" - 12"
Serving Forks   8" - 12"
Tongs   4", 6" 8"
One Piece Salad Servers

Determining the Reception Schedule

By filling in the following table you will have a schedule for the time line of your reception. This information will also be helpful to the disc jockey and the people setting up the buffet. This is just a guideline. The only items in the schedule that really need to take place at the designated times is the "I DO" and the "Goodnight".

Example	Start	Amt. of time
What time does wedding begine?	12:00	45 minutes
Length of wedding	12:45	45 minutes
Time needed by photographer following wedding	1:30	20 minutes
Time to travel from location of wedding ceremony to reception hall	1:50	15 minutes
The Beginning	Start	**Amt of time**
What time does the wedding begin?		
Length of wedding		
Time needed by photographer following wedding		
Time needed to travel from location of wedding ceremony to reception hall		
Reception Line -Optional - None of our clients have observed this custom, the bride and groom have preferred to mingle with the guests after they finished eating - prior to the toast.		
Food Service and dining		
Toasts		
First Dance		
Other Significant Dances (EX: Father with Bride, Groom with Mother)		
Cake Cutting		
Dancing		
Clean up		

BUFFET SET UP GUIDELINES

The room, the number of guests, the space available and the variety of dishes you will be serving will be key determining factors in the set up.

THE ROOM, SPACE & TRAFFIC FLOW

The first consideration is determining what area to use for the buffet. It should be close to the kitchen area, not on the opposite side of the room. If you will be serving from both sides of the table, you will need ample area for access. Plan on an area a minimum of 6' x 30' for the buffet. Remember to plan for an area for the guests standing in line, which is explored in more detail below.

If you are serving outdoors, the kitchen access should be close by.

We have found using two to three eight foot tables for a single line works well depending on the number of dishes you are serving. If your guest list exceeds 150, you will need two duplicate lines of food. They can be in separate areas, or you can set up a double length of table, have guests start at both ends (front and back), and have a common dish in the middle that will signify the end of the line. We were helping with a wedding for 300 and didn't have an inch to spare. We set up a 45' buffet with a huge bread roll waterfall in the middle for the centerpiece. The guests knew when they reached the rolls and the oncoming guests that they had reached the end of the selections. Using this arrangement, everyone was served in about 45 minutes.

Picture the traffic flow to the buffet area and guests returning to their tables. If you have a large room, the movement should be fairly uncomplicated. Try to avoid having everyone line up for the buffet at one time. Unless you are in a huge room, the result will be a long line impeding other guests returning to their tables. Instructing the DJ to direct specific tables to join the buffet line at intervals is the most effective tool we have seen to minimize this problem.

If you are dealing with multiple doorways just be aware that there could be congestion in these areas. The goal is to avoid the guests carrying plates having to cut across lines of those waiting to go thru the buffet. Consider having guests leave the room thru one doorway and re-enter thru another.

If you are holding your function in a private home or in a facility that cannot accommodate a single buffet table arrangement, set up smaller tables at various locations in the facility. If you select this option, consider traffic flow when you choose your menu. We have seen this used most effectively with appetizer and hors d'oeuvre selections.

The key to a buffet line moving smoothly is to serve the food in large dishes. This reduces the interruptions to the line moving as the food is replenished. We are found dishes with compatible shapes complement the presentation. Roughly, this translates to "don't mix square edges with rounds edges in serving pieces, with the exception of the chafing dishes". Ovals and rounds work well together and contribute to a lovely presentation.

Determine whether you will be using a centerpiece. It could be a flower arrangement, a colorful food presentation, or a cascading waterfall of rolls.

The only rule we follow rigidly is that the plates are placed at the beginning of the table, silverware and napkins at the end.

The factors that determine where to place the food on the table are:
The color and texture of the food
The type of serving dish
Menu item

We suggest placing the food as it would be served in a multiple course meal. The appetizers and salads would be served first and the entrée, vegetables and potato following that; which means the chafing dishes would be located near the end.

The exception to this guideline would be if you are serving a special dish. Recently we assisted at a wedding where the couple served a Green-Chile, Cheese, and Rice Casserole. Because they and their friends loved this dish, they had prepared a large quantity of the casserole. So, we put the chafing dish with this casserole at the beginning of the line. All the salads, rolls, meat, cheese, fruit and veggie platters followed. We wanted to make sure that there was plenty of room on the guest's plate for this dish, which there was.

If your menu does not follow the meat, veggie, potato scenario you will be able to be very creative. If you are serving salads and items arranged on trays; mix and match so your guests will see color and texture variation as they move down the table. If you are serving from both sides of the buffet; mirror the dishes so each side has a dish. Use footed cake plates to serve items that can be stacked on top of each other, this will add height to the presentation. If you use an elevated serving piece it can usually be easily accessed by both sides; therefore only one piece is needed rather than two to have the mirror effect.

If you are using an extremely large serving piece, such as a 23" salad bowl, it can easily be accessed by both sides. It can be placed with mirrored pieces preceding and following it to add visual interest to the table. Or place a single item at the beginning, all the mirrored pieces in a row, another single item followed by the chafers. The great thing about working with food presentation is that two of the design elements (color and texture) are inherent....you just need to move the dishes around unit they look balanced and: Viola!! You are finished.

The following diagram is an example just to give you an idea of a potential layout. You might be working with fewer salads, or only one meat. Determine how many chafers you will be using, where they will be placed and then use the other dishes to fill around them.

If you are looking through various bridal magazines watch for reception pictures of buffets. Granted they will probably be much more elaborate than what you want....but you can pick up lots of ideas.

If there are remaining appetizers use them to fill in any blank areas on the buffet. This is an example of a single line set-up with guests moving down the front and back of the table

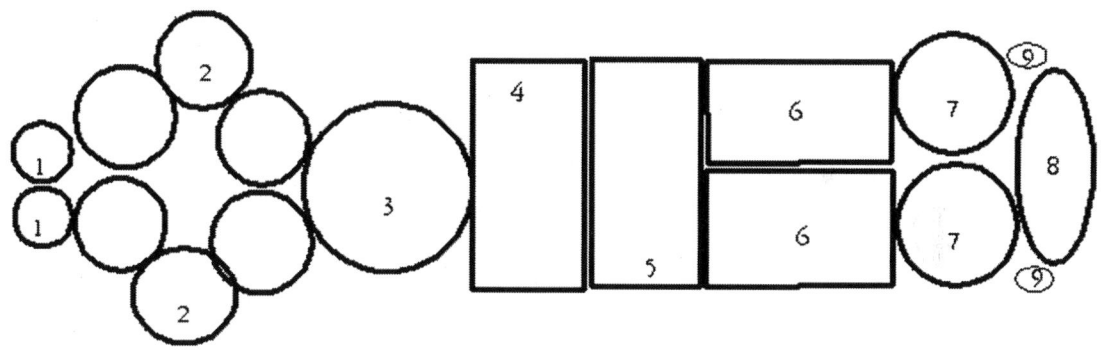

Key follows

1 Plates

2 3 types of salads (mirrored)

3 Fruit Plate (shared)

4 Potatoes   (shared)

5 Vegetable   (shared)

6 Meat   (mirrored)

7 Rolls   (mirrored)

8 Basket of individual servings of flatware pieces rolled in a napkin (shared)

9 Butter   (mirrored)

You can play with setting up your own diagram in Word
Use "Insert" function, drop down to "Auto Shapes" and double click to select a shape.
Position the cursor where you want the dish and click. You can modify shapes by
double clicking and then selecting the edge.
Repeat this for each dish you will have on the buffet.
Size the shape to represent the size of serving piece you will be using, and drag the
shapes to where you think a menu item will work well.
Use "Insert", "Text Box", size it as small as possible, drag to one of the shapes and then
double click to insert a number for the key. Repeat until each shape has a number
that will correspond to a menu item.

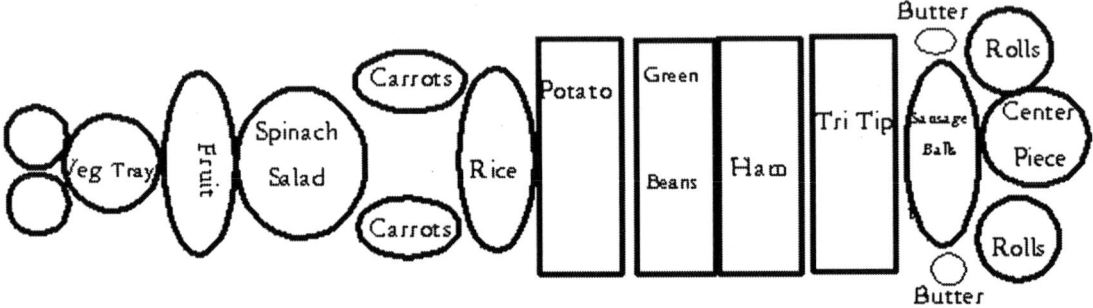

This is one half of the arrangement that was used to serve 300 guests.....the same
set up was mirrored on the right side of the table . The lines served from the front
and back which provided four lines of service. The line terminated at the rolls and
butter; when the guest met the oncoming guests at the rolls, they knew they were
at the "end of the line"

HELPFUL INFORMATION

The following pages contain reference information we suggest you review.
You might not actually need it, but you will know it is there.

Food Safety
Good hygiene habits when handling food are very important.
Our clients have never had any problems with guests becoming
ill during, or after, their functions.
We hope by paying attention to detail you will have the same experience.

Serving guests within the shortest time frame possible is desirable to
keep your function on schedule;
And, it has a major impact on the safety factor of the food you are serving.
That being said; also remember that you are not serving a buffet
that will be sitting out for several hours.
Most dishes will be replenished within ten to fifteen minutes of
being placed on the buffet.

Food Weight – Measurement Table for Common Food Items
How many ounces of chopped parsley do you need for ¾ of a cup?
How many peeled oranges equal a pound?
How many unpeeled oranges equal a pound?

Common Can Sizes
How much food is in a #10 can?

FOOD PREPARATION PRACTICES

Keep everything that touches food clean-utensils, pans, bowls, countertops, hands, gloves.

Wash hands before handling food, after handling raw food, and after touching anything that may contaminate food.

Use disposable gloved hands, tongs, or other methods to keep bare hands from touching ready-to-eat foods.

Use separate cutting boards and utensils for cooked and uncooked meat, poultry, and fish and for raw and ready-to-eat foods.

Keep juices from raw meat, poultry, and fish from contacting other foods.

Sanitize all utensils, pans, bowls, and food contact surfaces after being used for preparing potentially hazardous foods and before coming in contact with raw or ready-to-eat foods.

Serving - Keep potentially hazardous food either at or below 41°F or above 140°F. Take temperatures every 30 minutes.

When replenishing food on a buffet, do not mix fresh food with food that has been out for service.

Do not mix raw food with cooked food.

Use disposable gloved hands, tongs, or other methods to keep bare hands from touching read-to-eat foods.

Leftovers- Freeze or refrigerate leftovers immediately. Follow established guidelines for cooling food quickly. Reheat foods one time only.

Food Safety Information

Temperatures and bacteria growth

Temperature °F	Bacteria activity
212	Most bacteria destroyed
140 and above	Low survival rate, prevent bacteria growth
120-140	Survival and growth
60-120	Reproduce rapidly (99 degrees F ideal for growth)
40-140	Survival and growth
32-40	Slow growth rate

Safe internal temperatures for cooked foods

Food	Internal temperature

Poultry

Boneless, ground, stuffed	165 °F for 15 sec
Bone-in pieces	170 °F
Whole birds	180 °F

Ground/Chopped/Tenderized Meat

Beef, pork, sausage, lamb, fish	155 °F for 15 seconds (see Note)

Pork

Pork, ham	145 °F for 15 seconds

Beef/Veal/Lamb

Steaks, chops, roasts (see Notes)	145 °F for 15 seconds

Fish

Solid	145 °F for 15 seconds
Stuffed	165 °F

Other

Reheated foods	165 °F for 15 seconds (within 2 hr.)
Stuffed pasta, stuffed meat	165 °F for 15 seconds
Eggs	155 °F for 15 seconds
Dairy, pasta, grains, rice	145 °F for 15 seconds

Food serving temperatures and holding times

Food	Serving temp °F	Approximate holding time
Beverages		
Cold drinks-juices	40	30 minutes, if poured
Hot drinks	185	30-45 minutes
Coffee*	185	Hot plate,;20 minutes, Insulated pot; 2 hours

Dairy

Ice Cream	10	6-8 hours, dipped
Milk	34-38	

Desserts

Pudding and refrigerator		
Desserts	41 or less	
Pastries and cakes**	60-70	

Entrees, Soup

Beef, roast***	150	10-15 minutes
Casseroles, stews, soups	170-180	30-45 minutes
Chicken, baked	160	20-30 minutes
Eggs, scrambled	160	10-15 minutes
Ham, pork roast	160	10-15 minutes
Sandwiches, hot	160	10-15 minutes

Salads

All cold   41 or less

Sauces, Vegetables

Vegetables in cream sauce	145-160	15-30 Minutes
Vegetables unseasoned	160-170	15-20 Minutes
Whipped potatoes	160-170	15-20 Minutes

Methods for Cooling Hot Foods

A.   Procedure: Cut large food items into smaller pieces.
        Application: large roasts, whole poultry or fish
B.   Procedure: Pour hot, thick foods into clean, chilled shallow, stainless steel pans, to no more than
        2 inched deep.
        Application: stews, chili, pasta casseroles, pudding
C.   Procedure: Pour hot, thin foods into clean pans or pots, to no more than 3 inches deep.
        Application: broth soups, thin sauces
D.   Procedure: Set pan of food in an ice water bath (set pan with hot food inside another pan filled
        with ice) Stir both the hot food and the ice. Replace ice as it melts.
        Application: pourable thin or thick foods
E.   Procedure: Delete part of the water in the recipe and add ice in the cooling step. The weight of
        the ice should be equal to the water deleted from the recipe.
        Application: thick, pourable foods such as chili and pasta sauces that may be prepared, cooled,
        and heated
                        For service at a later time.

Methods for Chilling Cold Foods

A.   Chill ingredients thoroughly before combining (i.e., salad dressings, tuna, hard-cooked eggs, and
        canned kidney beans).
B.   Put dense products into clean, chilled, shallow, stainless steel pans to no more than 2 inches deep.

Notes: Hot foods will cool faster if loosely covered or uncovered. Protect uncovered food from
contamination.
        Cover food tightly after chilling.
        Allow air to circulate around pans. Do not stack pans.
        Stirring foods with a clean utensil once or twice during cooling can shorten chilling time.

Time and temperature standards for reducing food safety hazards of potentially hazardous foods

Step	Standard
Receiving	Frozen foods at 0°F or below
	Refrigerated foods at 41°F or below
Storage	Frozen foods at 0°F or below
	Refrigerated foods at 41°F or below for 7 calendar days or 45°F for 4 calendar days (The calendar day counting period begins as day 1 on the day the food is refrigerated.)

Thawing	In refrigerator at 41°F or below
	Under potable, running cold water (70°F or less) for not more than 2 hours

Food Production

Pre-preparation	Keep all PHF at 41°F or below or at 140°F or above throughout preparation time. Cool cooked products rapidly to 70°F within 2 hours and from 70°F to 41°F or below in 4 additional hours or less.
Preparation	*Cold Foods:* Rapid cooling to 41°F or below.
	Hot foods: Cook to internal temperatures specified in the recipe (reheated foods to 165°F). Maintain hot holding temperature at or above 140°F (see notes).
Postproduction	Cool leftover food rapidly to 70°F within 2 hours and from 70°F to 41°F or less in 4 additional hours or less. Store cooked food in clean shallow pans or containers that are no more than 4 inched deep with a product depth of no more than 2 inches. If product is thick, stir frequently until cooled.
Serving	Maintain internal temperature at 140°F or more or 41°F or less (see Notes). Do not mix old product with freshly cooked product.
Cooling	Cool rapidly to 70°F within 2 hours and from 70°F to 41°F or less in 4 additional hours or less. (see Postproduction).
Notes:	In some locations, regulatory agencies will permit time to be used as control rather than holding temperatures. For time to be used as a control, the following conditions must be met: (1) The product must be marked with the time it is removed from temperature control: and (2) the product will be cooked and served or discarded within 4 hours. Measure all temperatures with a cleaned and samiti8zed stem thermometer or thermocouple thermometer.

General Guidelines for Handling Food Safety

Cooking	Cook all meat to the required internal temperature to kill harmful organisms. Measure internal temperature in several places. Wash and sanitize thermometers after each use. Use an accurate thermometer or thermocouple to measure internal temperature of potentially hazardous foods. Do not rely on color for determining if meat, chicken or fish has reached the correct end-point temperature. Do not interrupt cooking by partially cooking potentially hazardous food and then finishing later. Return all potentially hazardous foods to refrigerator when preparation is interrupted. Work with small amount of food at a time to maintain safe temperature. Never mix old product with new.
Serving	Keep potentially hazardous food either at or below 41°F or above 140°F. Take temperatures every 30 minutes. When replenishing food on a buffet, do not mix fresh food with food that has been out for service. Do not mix raw food with cooked food. Use disposable gloved hands, tongs, or other methods to keep bare hands from touching read-to-eat foods.
Leftovers	Freeze or refrigerate leftovers immediately. Follow established guidelines for cooling food quickly. Reheat foods, one time only, to 165°F (within 2 hours).

Food Weight – Measure Equivalents

Food	Weight	Approximate measure
Apples	1 lb	3 medium
Apples, pared and diced, 1 ½-inch cubes	1 lb	2 ¾ cups
Avocado	1 lb	2 medium
Bananas	1 lb	3 medium
Beans, green, cut, cooked	1 lb	3 cups
Broccoli, florets	1 lb	4 cups
Broccoli, head	1 lb	1 medium
Butter	1 lb	2 cups
Cabbage, raw, shredded	1 lb	1 qt lightly packed
Cantaloupe	3 lb	1 melon, 6-inch diameter
Carrots, fresh	1 lb	4-5 medium
Cauliflower, florets	1 lb	4 cups
Cauliflower, head	1 lb	1 medium
Celery, diced	1 lb (1-2 bunches)	1 qt
Cheese, loaf, slices	1 lb	16-20 slices
Cheese, mozzarella Shredded	1 lb	3 ½ cups
Cherries, maraschino, drained	1 lb	50-60 cherries
Chicken, cooked, cubed	1 lb	3 cups
Chicken, ready to cook	4-4 ½ lb	1 qt cooked, diced
Cucumbers, sliced	1 lb	50-60 slices
Eggplant	1 lb	8 slices, 4 x ½ inch
Eggplant	1 lb	1 qt diced
Garlic, fresh	1 oz	6 large closes
Garlic, fresh, minced	1 oz	3 Tbsp
Ham, cooked, diced	1 lb	3 cups
Ham, cooked, ground	1 lb	2 ½ cups
Lemon juice	1 lb	2 cups (8-10 lemons)
Lemons,	1 lb	4-5 lemons yield ¾ cup juice
Lettuce, average head	2 lb	1 head
Lettuce, chopped shredded	1 lb	6-8 cups
Lettuce, leaf	1 lb	25-30 salad garnishes
Limes, fresh juice	1 lb	5 limes, 15-20 thin slices yield, 7/8 cup
Macaroni, 1 lb after cooking	3 lb	2-2 ¼ qt

Macaroni, cooked	1 lb	3 cups
Mushrooms, fresh, sliced	1 lb	5 cups raw (1 ¾ cups cooked)
Mustard, ground, dry	1 oz	5 Tbsp
Noodles cooked	1 lb	2 ¾ cups
Noodles, 1 lb, cooked	3 lbs	2 qt
Olives	1 lb	2/3 cup chopped
Olives, green, small size drained	1 lb	160 olives
Olives, green, stuffed	1 lb	2 ½ cups
Olives, ripe, sliced	1 lb	3 1/3 cups
Olives, ripe, Drained	1 lb	140 small, 110 medium 90 large olives
Onions, dehydrated	1 lb	8 lb raw (equivalent)
Onions, dehydrated	1 oz	5 Tbsp
Onions, fresh, chopped	1 lb	2 ½ - 3 cups
Onions, green, sliced	1 lb	2 ½ - 3 cups
Onions, mature	1 lb	4 – 5 medium
Oranges, medium	1 lb	3-4 oranges, unpeeled; 5 oranges, peeled; 10-11 sections each; yield, 1 cup juice
Parsley, coarsely chopped	1 oz	¾ cup
Peaches, fresh	1 lb	3 medium
Peppers, green	1 lb	2-3 medium
Peppers, green, chopped	1 lb	3 cups
Pineapple, fresh	2-4 lb	1 pineapple, 2-4 cups, cubed
Potatoes, fresh, white	1 lb	3 medium
Potatoes, fresh, white, cooked	1 lb	2 ½ cups
Potatoes, sweet	1 lb	3 medium
Potatoes, sweet, cooked	1 lb	2 cups
Radishes	1 lb	45-50
Raisins	1 lb	3 cups
Rice, brown	1 lb	2 ½ cups
Rice, converted	1 lb	2 ½ cups
Rice, cooked	1 lb	2 ¼ cups
Rice, 1 lb after cooking	3 ½ lb	2 qt
Rice, precooked	1 lb	4 ½ cups
Rice, regular	1 lb	2 ½ cups
Sausage, link, small	1 lb	1-17 link
Shrimp, cleaned, cooked peeled	1 lb	3 ¼ cups
Spaghetti, cooked	1 lb	2 2/3 cups
Spinach, raw	1 lb	5 qt lightly packed
Spinach, raw, chopped	1 lb	3 ¼ qt
Strawberries, fresh or Frozen	1 lb	3 cups

Tomatoes, fresh	1 lb	2-3 medium, 12 slices
Tomatoes, fresh plum	1 lb	6 medium
Tortillas, flour	10 inch	1 lb 9
Watermelon	1 lb	1-inch slice, 6 inch diameter

Common Can Sizes

Can size (industry term)	Approximate net weight or fluid measure	Approximate cups per can	Approximate number of 4-oz portions	Principal products
No 10	6lb/7lb 5 oz	9-12	25	Institutional size for Fruits, vegetables
No. 5 Squat	4-4 ¼ lb	8	16-20	Institutional size for Canned fish, sweet potatoes
No 3 Cyl	46 fl oz or 51 fl oz	5 ¼	10-12	Fruit and vegetable juices, condensed soups
No. 2 ½	26-30 oz	3 ½	5-7	Fruits, some vegetables
No 2	18 fl oz or 20 fl oz	2 ½	5	Juices, fruits ready-to-serve soups
No. 303	1 lb	2	4	Fruits, vegetables, ready-to Serve soups
No. 300	14-16 oz	1 ¾	3-4	Some fruits and meat products
No 1 (Picnic)	10 ½-12 oz	1 ¼	2-3	Condensed soups
8 oz	8 oz	1	2	Read-to-serve soups, fruits, vegetables

Note   When substituting one can for another size, one No. 10 can is approximately equivalent to:
7 No 303 (1lb) cans
5 No. 2 (1lb 4 oz) cans
4 No. 2 ½ (1lb 13 oz) cans
2 No. 3 (46 to 50 oz) cans

INDEX

Made in the USA
Charleston, SC
20 July 2010